**Dr Julian and Mrs
Marianna Kennedy**
77 Muroo Park, Ballymena
Co. Antrim BT43 6JQ

CW00971424

LIVING
JOYFULLY
in
Marriage

LIVING JOYFULLY
in
Marriage

REFLECTING THE
RELATIONSHIP *of*
CHRIST *and the*
Church

STEVEN KEY

REFORMED
FREE PUBLISHING
ASSOCIATION
Jenison, Michigan

All Bible quotations are taken from the King James [Authorized] Version

Reformed Free Publishing Association
1894 Georgetown Center Drive
Jenison MI 49428
616-457-5970
www.rfpa.org
mail@rfpa.org

Cover design by Erika Kiel
Interior design by Katherine Lloyd / theDESKonline.com

ISBN: 978-1-944555-95-5
ISBN: 978-1-944555-96-2 (ebook)
LCCN: 2021948289

To my wife, Nancy, with whom

I have been blessed by God

to live joyfully in marriage since 1976.

Contents

Introduction

This book has its roots with encouragement by the elders of Loveland Protestant Reformed Church and some of the members of the congregation, where the contents of this book were first presented in a series of sermons in 2015. This material is important not only for married couples—because then many people would be excluded—but for everyone.

Premarital counseling has been tremendously beneficial toward establishing strong, healthy marriages in Christ's church. But not everyone has had that benefit when establishing their marriages. In addition, premarital counseling is not a cure-all. As I emphasize in those counseling sessions, if you are not going to lay hold by faith and to apply the instruction of God's word to your marriage, you are not going to enjoy God's blessing in your marriage. If your marriage is suffering, don't point the finger at your spouse, but look deeply at yourself in the light of God's word.

There is clearly a need for the strengthening of our marriages, so that we might live rightly and joyfully in, and not defile, the glorious relationship that is to reflect Christ and the church. In some cases, it may be necessary that we not perpetuate but forsake the sins we observed in our homes growing up. In other cases, we must repent of a very selfish and improper view of marriage. But in all cases, we must devote ourselves to being *doers* of the word, not just hearers.

Marriage problems are as old as the fall into sin by the first married couple, Adam and Eve. But we live in a period of history where the assaults upon marriage are unrelenting. Because of marriage's critical importance to the church, and because of what it stands for and represents, namely, the glorious relationship between Christ and his church, no institution is under such open and fierce and relentless attack in our day as the institution of marriage.

There is a war tactic called "saturation bombardment" when every means is used to bomb the enemy relentlessly until he collapses. To those who reject God's truth *we* are the enemy. And in our day they are using every means—including all the media, especially television and all that is accessible via the internet, political processes, and more—to undermine what the Bible calls *holy* marriage.

That began already in the early years of television, what some refer to as the "years of innocence," when husbands began to be portrayed as incompetent buffoons and women were the ones who really ran the household. But sin develops.

The sexual revolution of the 1960s showed the astounding speed of the development of sin, a speed that only continues to increase at an explosive rate, as if mankind would see marriage dissolved in a giant sonic boom.

Sexual purity or chastity within the holy bond of marriage is rejected openly. Unmarried men and women shaking their fists at God and living together without shame is common today and accepted by society at large. We are told by the media and by politicians and social leaders and psychologists and others that sexual activity outside of marriage—which belongs to what the Bible calls the *sin* of fornication—is a part of growing up today and should be promoted, but with certain safety precautions.

Adultery is such a common phenomenon today that people in the public eye no longer have to pay a price of shame, let alone removal from office, for such violation of God's law. The sanctity of marriage and its permanence is ridiculed, with easy divorce and remarriage being advocated as the solution to marriage problems.

So astounding has been sin's development that there is a

widespread cry today to attempt to *redefine* marriage, as permitting same-sex couples—a redefinition now established by the courts and by our institutions of government.

When it comes to God's ordinance that a man and wife bring forth children, the world levels its vicious attack against God's people who would bring forth large families while at the same time giving approval to the mass murder of unborn children, slaying millions in the United States alone with abortion on demand. In this way also the ungodly would turn us against that which God has ordained and the way in which he is pleased to bring forth his church.

Then there is the more underlying factor that views even relationships from a perspective of self-seeking and pleasure. "What's the benefit to me?"

The spiritual attacks are intense!

Sadly, the church has already succumbed to these attacks of Satan from many perspectives.

This is not even to take into account our own sinfulness and our own personal attacks upon this holy relationship by our mistreatment of our spouses, our sinful behavior within this relationship, our frequent departures from the Bible's instruction, in which we attack *our own happiness*. Our own marriages are at stake! That is evident by the number of marriages in the church that are not what they *must* be before God.

And while the church is called to receive with open arms those who are led by God to repent of such sins, and while Paul writes, "And such were some of you: but ye are washed, but ye are sanctified, but ye are justified in the name of the Lord Jesus, and by the Spirit of our God" (1 Cor. 6:11), the fact remains, it is for these reasons—and we could mention many others—that we need to know God's word concerning marriage and the family, and in obedience to God live as he would have us live.

To that end, the instruction we turn to in God's word is intended to remind us how marriage is to be *lived*.

It is not my intention to repeat the foundational series that Prof. David Engelsma preached years ago in Loveland at a time when marriage problems were also evident, which sermons were published in the book *Marriage: The Mystery of Christ and the Church*.[1] Although I highly recommend this book, my approach is going to be different. While beginning with the divine institution of marriage, and not overlooking the foundational truths of the role of a husband, the role of a wife, and so on, I intend to focus on what it is to live joyfully in marriage.

In outlining that main theme and selecting texts, I have divided the book into three main sections. The first sub-section of my main theme will be what I am calling "Essentials to Joyful Marriage." That will be followed by four chapters under another sub-section entitled "Privileged to Make It Work." Then will follow several chapters under the final sub-section, "Dedicated to Expressing the Joy," or what might also be referred to as "Bringing Christ's Life to Expression in Marriage."

Summarized: I want you to understand what marriage is and what it requires for those who are redeemed by Christ's precious blood. What God has taught us is what is *best* for us and for our joy in the fellowship of his love.

Because this book is going to deal much with relationships, I trust it will be beneficial in ways that apply to more than just the marriage relationship.

Not to be overlooked in this book is the glory of single life. Single life is not a curse, and it is not a disease. It must be viewed as a glorious calling for some. In addition, because we are members of one body, it is important that our single members—even those who

---

1   David J. Engelsma, *Marriage: The Mystery of Christ and the Church* (Jenison, MI: Reformed Free Publishing Association, 2014).

have been bereaved and those who have been forsaken by a spouse, as well as our unmarried young adults and young people—have a *biblical* understanding of marriage.

We all must uphold that divine institution, no matter our personal situation in life. But especially for the sake of our children, our marriages must reflect the relationship between Christ and the church. God would have us live joyfully in marriage, that our children might understand from that example that the Christian life in fellowship with our Lord Jesus Christ is a life of joy, in which we delight in the intimacy of fellowship with God. That, after all, alone can provide our children the stability that they need for a life of joy in God's covenant.

I want you to see that also single life is lived in the midst of Christ's church as belonging to *the* marriage of the church to Christ. After all, when God instituted marriage to reflect his great love for us in Christ Jesus, he not only taught us *what* marriage must be, but he made marriage a help to our understanding of the gospel and to our own place in relationship to Christ.

In addition, we must remember that the chief enemy of marriage, also *our* enemy as members of Christ's bride, is that of sinful self-centeredness, or pride. That is why, when we speak about living joyfully in marriage and consider many of the biblical teachings concerning relationships, which teachings are essential to healthy, joyful marriages, we are standing before truths that apply also to all healthy relationships within the bride of Christ.

So besides growing in our understanding of marriage, we will benefit from God's word pertaining to our relationship to Christ and to one another. Whether as husband or wife, or in the higher calling as partakers of the marriage between Christ and his church, I would have you maintain and enjoy this relationship, as redeemed and sanctified and brought under the dominion of Christ and his word.

But I also remind you of the words of James 1:22. The Christian, in hearing the word of God, does not just say, "Nice word; we need to hear that," and continue to walk his or her own way. If so, that person's Christianity is self-deception, James bluntly tells us. We must be *doers* of the word. When you hear what God says concerning marriage, then by God's grace and the work of his Spirit in your heart, you put to practice what you hear and glorify your Redeemer who has taken you as his bride.

Steven R. Key

Part I

Essentials to Joyful Marriage

●

Chapter 1

THE ESSENCE OF JOY: MARRIAGE TO CHRIST

3. That which we have seen and heard declare we unto you, that ye also may have fellowship with us: and truly our fellowship is with the Father, and with his Son Jesus Christ.
4. And these things write we unto you, that your joy may be full.—1 John 1:3–4

I have entitled this first section of the book "Essentials to Joyful Marriage." That is the expression that came to mind because the recognition of these truths and living in the consciousness of these truths is necessary for holding any marriage together and for keeping the bands of joy attached to that marriage.

The first thing necessary for a book entitled *Living Joyfully in Marriage* is to consider the meaning of joy. After all, which couple upon getting married does not want a joy-filled marriage? But the idea of joy in marriage is often defined by a very selfish perspective. What can I get out of this relationship? In what way will this fulfill me? Joy is mistakenly viewed in terms of getting what I want. Such a view will inevitably leave one disappointed and disillusioned. So we must establish from the very beginning that joy in marriage is not a personal happiness found in self-fulfillment. It is something far deeper and profoundly beautiful.

Galatians 5:22 identifies the second manifestation of the fruit of the Spirit as *joy*. What a blessing to be partakers of that fruit, to live as Christians in the joy that is ours in Christ Jesus! Joy is ours—as we learn especially from John's first epistle—as we live in the fellowship of our Redeemer. So the fruit of the Spirit is fruit that we enjoy and that we bear *in Christ* and in the consciousness of our marriage to him. We need to be aware of the wonder of our union with Christ. We need to be reminded of that truth constantly.

Our great adversary, Satan, and those whom he has deceived are doing everything possible to bring ruin to God's cause. He can never do so successfully. Christ is already victorious. At the cross and especially by his resurrection from the dead, Christ conquered the prince of this world. But that defeated devil continues to thrash around, asserting himself in the vain attempt to devour Christ's bride, the church. He does so especially by attempting to disrupt our fellowship with God and to defile our relationship as those married to Christ. Increasingly in our day the unbelieving world shows its hatred toward Christ and his church. Belonging to that hatred are the attacks upon marriage as the reflection of the relationship between Christ and his bride. Our lives as Christians are influenced by and affected by those attacks. Some succumb to them.

The Holy Spirit through the inspired apostle John sets before us the beautiful balance of the Christian life as it comes to expression in this fallen world. Living in fellowship with God, we walk with a spiritual focus and therefore show ourselves spiritually separate, children of the light living in the midst of darkness. In spite of the dangers and in spite of the sinfulness of our own natures against which we battle constantly, we have life eternal, fellowship with the Father and with his Son Jesus Christ. This truth, a matter of our own experience by the Spirit's work, is the source of triumphant joy. So John writes.

After having introduced his epistle by pointing us to the Christ in whom is life eternal, and therefore to the blessedness of the covenantal life that is fellowship with God, the inspired apostle says, "And these things write we unto you, that your joy may be full" (1 John 1:4). His desire is that these believers to whom he writes—and the Spirit has preserved this for us—might have fullness of joy, even though we live in a world full of difficulties, trials, and sorrows. The apostle John testified of the gospel of our fellowship with God and with his Son Jesus Christ. Without using the specific language, he testified of our marriage to Christ. He did so with the express purpose that your joy may be full. He could not have written these words without remembering the words of the Lord Jesus that he had recorded in his gospel account: "These things have I spoken unto you, that my joy might remain in you, and that your joy might be full" (John 15:11). Christ has spoken to us that his joy might remain in us, and our joy might be full. But what is meant by that reference to joy?

Joy

When you take into account the words of Jesus in John 15:11 and look more closely at 1 John 1:3–4, you must realize that joy belongs to the very essence of the Christian life. The Christian has joy. It might be obscured, and often is. We look for the fullness of it. But that joy is ours in Christ Jesus. It belongs to the very essence of Christianity, to our marriage union with Christ.

It is noteworthy that as John wrote these words he was standing on the threshold of his last agony. Humanly speaking, we would say that it was hardly a time for great joy for the apostle. He was a very aged saint. As we age, we long more and more for heaven. We don't know what afflictions the apostle bore as the marks of his old age, but we know that with age comes affliction, the breakdown of the body. We experience it. Married couples also realize that their earthly relationship is soon to come to its end. We attend a wedding, the beginning of a marriage in the Lord, and would describe that event with the adjective *joyful*. It is a time of joy. That term does not generally come to mind when we stand before the divine parting of the marriage relationship in death.

We also know that John was laboring at a time when the church was under fierce attack. He refers to that in his letter. As pastors always bear the brunt of being on the foreground in such attacks, being most aware of them and most distracted by them, we would not think of John at such a moment in his life as being characterized by great joy. But he meets what conflicts and trials and afflictions he must bear with a joy that he must convey to Christ's church. The fullness of joy that he experiences, he would have you experience.

This text therefore stands as a stark reminder that as Christians our focus is out of place when we persist in a chronic state of melancholy or despair. You realize, I trust, even before we get to a positive treatment of what this joy is, that this joy is not simply something superficial, nor does it eliminate the reality of sorrow and tears. There is a time to weep, as we are told in Ecclesiastes 3:4. There is a time for the Christian even to be cast into sorrow. I speak not merely of the *natural* sorrow that is the result of death, the death of a spouse or a child for example. Such sorrow is an expression of *love*—although we must be careful that it is not the sorrow of despair. But the child of God may be and ought to be cast into deep sorrow over his or her falls into sin. "For godly sorrow worketh repentance to salvation not to be repented of," as we read in 2 Corinthians 7:10, "but the sorrow of the world worketh death." When we fall into sin, and God so works to open our eyes and see his holiness, there is a time for holy despair, godly sorrow. When Scripture calls us to "Rejoice evermore," as we read in 1 Thessalonians 5:16, or "Rejoice in the Lord always: and again I say, Rejoice" (Phil. 4:4), that does not mean there is no place for sorrow or tears. There is. But what the text reveals is that the Christian life may not be characterized by chronic despair and gloom.

Now this is where the background of the text is so vitally important. This entire epistle takes into account the dreadful difficulty of living in such a world as is in the bondage of death. When we, as Christians, understand the biblical perspective of things, then we have a realistic perspective of life in this world. Nor do we merely look on the surface of things, but we dig deeper, looking at the core, at the foundation of what we readily observe. We see death as the wages of sin. We understand that this world isn't getting better, nor may we expect it to get better. The development of sin that we observe, even the apostasy that marks the church and grows like a cancer, is evidence of the wrath of God revealed from heaven against all ungodliness and unrighteousness of men. We live in an evil world; and the temptations increase, also when it comes to upholding the sanctity of marriage. Moreover, we often stumble and fall. There are many sorrows. The same was true among those to whom John wrote. It is true for you and me.

But with what God has revealed to us by his gospel, we have no right to a sense of hopelessness and despair. In fact, to live that way is sin, a rejection of the precious promises of God and the testimony of his faithfulness. There are always those in the church who need to examine themselves in this connection. Always complaining, living in bitterness toward God, maybe even toward a husband or a wife, they seem to enjoy misery. But the apostle Paul, who wrote, "O wretched man that I am" (Rom. 7:24), also wrote, "Rejoice in the Lord always: and again I say, Rejoice" (Phil. 4:4). One of the manifestations of the fruit of the Spirit is joy. Where that is cast aside, there is a grieving of the Holy Spirit. This is because we so quickly take our focus off the Lord Christ and the wonder of grace and put it on ourselves. We turn our thoughts inward and become self-centered. We rob ourselves of the joy that ought to be our experience. Joy belongs to the Christian life because joy honors God. Therefore, we ought never give the impression that to be a Christian is an unhappy thing.

That being said, what *is* this joy?

Again, before looking at it positively, let's understand that this joy is not an attitude of flippancy, a cheap rosy outlook that is instilled by some self–pep talk. Nor is this joy some sudden outburst of emotion, rising up upon a surprise that prospers and makes happy, but soon to subside into a cold indifference. Of such the wise preacher wrote in Ecclesiastes 7:6, when he said, "As the crackling of thorns under a pot, so is the laughter of the fool." Sadly, that is the only type of joy the world will ever know.

When we talk about marriage, we need to realize that there is no real joy except as a fruit of the Spirit, from life in Christ. While the world might show a certain expression of happiness or joy, we must not fall into the mistake of thinking that their pleasures and their pleasantries are an expression of true joy. They aren't. The Bible acknowledges that there are pleasures to be found even in the way of sin. Those pleasures are not the seeds of joy, but of deepest sorrow. Those pleasures of sin are only for a season and result in death. This joy of which the apostle speaks isn't even dependent upon outward circumstances. Nor is this joy some superficial religious lightheartedness.

This joy is an expression of living in fellowship with God. It is an act of love that flows out of love for God, that first manifestation of the fruit of the Spirit. The fellowship with God that is ours by the Holy Spirit's work in our hearts arises out of a true knowledge of God and faith in our Lord Jesus Christ. Joy is an expression of our marriage to Christ and the knowledge of God's love for us in Christ. It is the knowledge of faith that we, of all people, have been given by God and taken by Christ as his bride. It is eternal life in the bonds of his covenantal embrace.

Because God has also taken his entire church in Christ into his own covenantal life of fellowship and love, we have fellowship not only with God, but with his people. Life in the covenant, the consciousness of God's fellowship in Jesus Christ, the fervent love for him that arises out of this wonder work of his grace in us by his Holy Spirit, instills in us the joy that Christ himself enjoys and that is ours by virtue of our union with him.

This joy, therefore, has several elements.

First, joy is a state of recognizing that we live in the fellowship of God's love for us in Christ. That means that a husband and wife must be able to make this confession together! As one flesh, they must be able to confess together, he is the God of our salvation! That's the heart of joy in marriage. The same is true of every person who is united to Christ by faith, a member of his bride. Joy is found in confessing from the heart, he is the God of my salvation! That is the testimony of the Holy Spirit in our hearts and minds by faith in Christ Jesus. In his Son God has revealed himself as Jehovah-salvation, who is unchangeably faithful in his love and tender mercy. Think of how many married couples you know who have faced great trials, even tragedies, or serious afflictions. In marriage you face those trials together, as two who are one. But you face them knowing the Lord's presence.

Whatever our circumstances in life, however great our troubles and sorrows, no matter how dark is the hour, he never forsakes us. Indeed, when everything appears to be against us, he is working for us, saving us, even through our afflictions. Not only has he told us so, but he has proven it through all ages in his dealings with his people and in our own lives in his dealings with us. And when we, who are miserable sinners, look upon this great God and see his love for us in Christ, we rejoice in him and in the fellowship of his love.

Second, let us remember, as Jesus taught us in John 15:26, the Spirit always testifies of Christ. This joy, therefore, because it finds its focus in Christ, is the knowledge and expression of victorious jubilation. This stands inseparably related to the first element of this joy, namely, that of recognizing that we live in the fellowship of God's love for us in Christ.

When I speak of joy in terms of victorious jubilation, it ought to be evident that this joy does not have its foundation in ourselves, in our life, in outward things, in a righteousness that is of the law. Marriage, after all, is marred by sin, something that we will consider throughout the chapters that follow. For our marriages to reflect the mystery of Christ and the church, we are called to the hard work of obedience to God's perfect instruction concerning our callings in every aspect of marriage. That calling, that labor, continues for our entire earthly sojourn. It continues until we are taken to heaven. If joy was to be established upon how well we live and how good we have been in our marriages, our joy would soon be consumed by the overwhelming reality of sin.

But when your focus is on God's great gift to you, when your focus is on Christ and the shedding of his blood, the pouring out of his life, the satisfaction of God's justice in your place and on your behalf; when you see that it was your righteousness that was sealed by his resurrection from the dead, so that your sins are blotted out and your adoption into God's family is sure, that he has poured out his Spirit upon you, that you of all people are a member of Christ's bride, then your joy is an expression of victorious exultation. It is the expression of thankfulness that cannot be held back. Rejoicing in him, you sing with gladness of heart that your names are written in heaven! That is exactly what the apostle Peter says when, pointing us to Christ, he says in 1 Peter 1:8, "Whom having not seen, ye love; in whom, though now ye see him not, yet believing, ye rejoice with joy unspeakable and full of glory." With a focus upon God and his Christ, we are marked by victorious jubilation. Joy unspeakable and full of glory! What a blessed fruit of the Spirit!

Third, when considering the elements of this joy, we find that belonging to this joy is a spiritual strength. On the observance of the feast of tabernacles after the return from the captivity, we find that God's law was proclaimed to the spiritual understanding of God's people. We read about it in Nehemiah 8. When the people of God saw themselves in the light of God's law, they were overwhelmed by the deep sense of their own guilt and sinfulness. We read, in fact, that the people broke down and wept "when they heard the words of the law" (v. 9). But Ezra pointed the people to their Messiah, commanding them to partake of the feast that the Lord had prepared them, "Neither be ye sorry; for the joy of the LORD is your strength" (v. 10). From the sorrow for their own guilt and sin, they were to look to Jehovah, their Savior—"for the joy of the LORD is your strength." Where would we be, if not for that?

In Psalm 5:11–12, the call is proclaimed, "But let all those that put their trust in thee rejoice: let them ever shout for joy, because thou defendest them: let them also that love thy name be joyful in thee. For thou, LORD, wilt bless the righteous; with favour wilt thou compass him as with a shield." There is nothing superficial about this joy. In this joy of the Lord, there is strength. When you are joyful, you are carried by a dynamic power, ready to meet every trial without losing hope, including every trial in married life. That is the Holy Spirit's work in you!

Fourth, this joy is an act of the will, for throughout Scripture we are called to rejoice. We must exercise ourselves in this act of rejoicing, keeping a proper spiritual focus with our eyes upon our heavenly Father and the Lord Jesus Christ. When we call attention to this particular element of the Christian's joy, we do not overlook nor minimize the fact, as with every aspect of our sanctification, that "it is God which worketh in you both to will and to do of his good pleasure" (Phil. 2:13). But "rejoice evermore" is the calling of the Christian. Key to this exercise of the will is the calling of Philippians 4:6–7, "Be careful for nothing; but in every thing by prayer and supplication with thanksgiving let your requests be made known unto God. And the peace of God, which passeth all understanding, shall keep your hearts and minds through Christ Jesus."

You understand, therefore, that the joy of which John writes is something very deep and profound. It affects the way we think and our approach to all of life. It affects our perspective of marriage as well, understanding that marriage reflects the relationship between Christ and his bride. This is the joy that comes from drawing water out of the wells of salvation, to use the language of Isaiah 12:3. In other words, it comes down to this: joy, as the fruit of the Spirit, is the response of the soul to a knowledge of the Lord Jesus Christ and the intimacy of our fellowship with him, our marriage to him.

The Fullness of This Joy

First John 1:4 calls our attention to the fact that this joy is to be *full* in us. What is the idea expressed in that desire that your joy be full?

The expression implies that we possess this joy in a measure. To know Christ, to be a partaker of his life, is to possess joy. We might easily get the impression from the text that the implication is, further, that while we have this joy, it is not yet full. We have it only in a small measure. But while that can sometimes be true, that is not the emphasis here. The tense of the verb used in the text speaks of a fullness that is already our possession. The idea is actually this: "These things write we unto you, that your joy may *remain full*." Not that it may be, or become, but that it may *remain* full.

Many things in our lives and many events we face would cause us to take our eyes off the source of our joy. Marriage, with all its activities and all its responsibilities, can distract us from the necessary nurture of our spiritual life with Christ. Our weak, sinful flesh is susceptible to losing spiritual focus and therefore detracting from the joy that is ours in Christ. There is a reason why the apostle Paul wrote:

32. But I would have you without carefulness. He that is unmarried careth for the things that belong to the Lord, how he may please the Lord:

33. But he that is married careth for the things that are of the world, how he may please his wife.

34. There is a difference also between a wife and a virgin. The unmarried woman careth for the things of the Lord, that she may be holy both in body and in spirit: but she that is married careth for the things of the world, how she may please her husband. (1 Cor. 7:32–34)

Those who are not married certainly have their own distractions. But marriage and family life can very easily distract us from our chief relationship, the marriage to Christ that is the source of all joy.

If we set aside for a moment the stark reality of our own sinfulness and look simply at the weakness of our human nature, we can look at Jesus for an example here. His whole earthly sojourn was filled with tormenting trials of his joy. Think of what it was like for him to look around in his family and see his own family members rejecting him. How many of us don't experience trials in our families, even in rejection of the truth or departures from the faith? And what grievous sin tears at the joy that ought to mark a Christian home! Jesus experienced the same in a way that you and I cannot even imagine, because he knew that he himself would bear the agonies of hell for his own loved ones. The Bible speaks of the sorrows that he bore in the contradiction of sinners against himself. We are told also of the exhaustion of his nature, a weariness that would almost compel him to say, "I can't go on!"

We could multiply examples of those things Jesus faced in his human nature that—though he was without sin, yet in the weakness of his human nature—would rob him of the fullness of joy. Yet we read that in one particularly dark hour, when he was facing the rejection of multitudes, "In that hour Jesus rejoiced in spirit" (Luke 10:21). We ask with amazement, "How is that possible?" But the answer is revealed in the rest of that text: "In that hour Jesus rejoiced in spirit, and said, I thank thee, O Father, Lord of heaven and earth, that thou hast hid these things from the wise and prudent, and hast revealed them unto babes: even so, Father; for so it seemed good in thy sight." You see? The joy of the Lord is his strength. Christ looks to his heavenly Father, being perfectly subject to his will, and says, "Thou art good! Thou doest all things in perfect wisdom." That was his strength; that was his joy. He placed his focus on God, who does that which is good in his sight. And what God does is good and right—because it is for the salvation of his church.

But Christ possessed the fullness of joy because he was emptied of self, to seek his Father and his Father's will. How necessary this is in marriage! We are so full of self, so self-centered. "Let this mind be in you, which was also in Christ Jesus: who, being in the form of God, thought it not robbery to be equal with God: but made himself of no reputation, and took upon him the form of a servant" (Phil. 2:5–7). "Husbands, love your wives, even as Christ also loved the church, and gave himself for it" (Eph. 5:25). Setting aside our worship of self, to seek our Father and Father's will, to live out of the knowledge of our faith union with Christ, is the way in which we rejoice—not only in God's fellowship, but in our fellowship with one another, also as husbands and wives.

John's desire is that your joy may remain full. You who are Christ's possess the joy of covenantal fellowship with God, adoption into his family with all the riches that his family life entails. But we tend to wander. We tend to lose focus; we tend to take our eyes off our Father and get all caught up in ourselves. Especially when we face trials of life and we focus our thoughts inward and it all becomes a matter of self and my troubles and my sorrows—me, me, me—the joy of fellowship with Christ is sucked right out of our life. We find ourselves miserable. That's what self-centeredness does. No true joy is or can be selfish. We need to be taken out of our narrow focus on self, out of the bondage and unbearable burden of our self-pity and self-inflicted loss of joy, and taken into Christ and into the loving fellowship of our heavenly Father, who would have us cast our burdens upon him.

To that end we have *Christ* set before us! To that end the gospel, good news, is declared—God having mercy upon us. He sees our needs every day and gives us one day a week in the office of the Great Physician, that in his house on the Lord's day, under the preaching of his word, we might be renewed in strength, even called to repentance, and restored to the fullness of joy. That is the significance also of Jesus' words in John 15:11: "These things have I spoken unto you, that my joy might remain in you, and that your joy might be full." Nor is this something only for heaven. It is evident that John is speaking of something that is and must be a present reality. For the life that we live as the children of God is a life that must reflect the life of Christ, in whom is fullness of joy.

The Source of This Joy

John 15:11 also points us to the source of this joy. Christ himself and his work for us and word to us is the source of this fullness of joy. To put it another way: the source of joy is our fellowship with the Father and with his Son Jesus Christ, by the work of the Holy Spirit. The fullness of joy comes in that measure of the knowledge of Christ by faith. In him, who is our life by his Spirit, is our fellowship with the Father and with all those who are his, including that spouse to whom I am married.

Here again is that which sets apart the Christian faith and life from every other teaching or religion. Our faith and life is that of a glorious relationship with God, fellowship in his covenantal life through Jesus Christ and by the work of the Holy Spirit. As the doctrine of election is the heart of the church, and the truth of the cross is the heart of the gospel, so a proper understanding of God's covenant is the heart of all true religion. And the only way into that relationship of covenantal fellowship with God is through Christ.

He is the beginning and the end. There is no true joy apart from him. In him we have life. Through him and by his Spirit alone we have access unto God. That is why, if we are to live in the fullness of joy, also in marriage, our spiritual life must be strong. We must continually see to the nurture and strength of our spiritual lives and "grow in grace, and in the knowledge of our Lord and Saviour Jesus Christ" (2 Pet. 3:18).

Christ himself ministers this fullness of joy to us also in our marriages through the preaching of his word applied by the Holy Spirit. So he nourishes and cherishes us, sanctifying and cleansing us (Eph. 5:26–29). Joy, after all, is a matter of the *conscious possession* of eternal life. That is given us by the Holy Spirit through the gospel. "These things write we unto you," says John (1 John 1:4). The *we* refers to the apostles, who wrote these things under the inspiration of the Holy Spirit. This is the word of God. This is the word that by the gospel is preached unto you. Let us understand then, not the Bible itself, not even the preaching of the word in itself, but the word of Christ used under the powerful influence of the Spirit of Christ is the cause of our joy. By the work of the Spirit through the word, we confess with Jeremiah in Jeremiah 15:16, "Thy words were found, and I did eat them; and thy word was unto me the joy and rejoicing of mine heart: for I am called by thy name, O LORD God of hosts." Notice that. By the word we receive the joy and rejoicing of knowing that we are called by the name of Jehovah God of hosts! We live in the fellowship of his love, and nothing can separate us from that love.

We bear in our lives the fruit of the Spirit! What a blessing! The Lord knows that we are flesh. He knows that our joy is often lacking, and sometimes even missing. Sometimes it is lacking because we are looking in the wrong place for that joy. Lot looked for it in the opportunities of Sodom; Samson looked for it in Delilah; Solomon in all kinds of women; the rich fool in his possessions. Some young people look for their joy in "good times" and even in the pleasures of sin that are for a season. Some look for joy in relationships, sometimes even in relationships that break fellowship with God. And God knows that a lack of watchfulness and prayer in our lives leaves us susceptible to a grievous fall into sin where there is such a loss of fellowship with God that we sense no joy.

So the Lord gives us his gospel. "And these things write we unto you, that your joy may be full" (1 John 1:4). As the Spirit gives us to see that in the midst of this darkness we have light in the Lord Jesus, he also produces in us and sustains in us the true and lasting joy of the Christian life. The same is true for marriage. Truly our fellowship is with the Father, and with his Son Jesus Christ. What greater joy can there be? Many might be the difficulties of our lives, heavy the burdens and sorrows. But Christ is the same, and his joy is the same. And in him you are kept, "whom having not seen, ye love; in whom, though now ye see him not, yet believing, ye rejoice with joy unspeakable and full of glory" (1 Pet. 1:8).

Chapter 2

THE DIVINE INSTITUTION OF MARRIAGE

18. And the LORD God said, It is not good that the man should be alone; I will make him an help meet for him.

19. And out of the ground the LORD God formed every beast of the field, and every fowl of the air; and brought them unto Adam to see what he would call them: and whatsoever Adam called every living creature, that was the name thereof.

20. And Adam gave names to all cattle, and to the fowl of the air, and to every beast of the field; but for Adam there was not found an help meet for him.

21. And the LORD God caused a deep sleep to fall upon Adam, and he slept: and he took one of his ribs, and closed up the flesh instead thereof;

22. And the rib, which the LORD God had taken from man, made he a woman, and brought her unto the man.

23. And Adam said, This is now bone of my bones, and flesh of my flesh: she shall be called Woman, because she was taken out of Man.

24. Therefore shall a man leave his father and his mother, and shall cleave unto his wife: and they shall be one flesh.

25. And they were both naked, the man and his wife, and were not ashamed.—Genesis 2:18–25

G od himself instituted and established marriage as a good, even
beautiful relationship between one man and one woman as
long as they both shall live. In doing so, God formed marriage to
reflect his own glorious covenantal life of fellowship and love, a relationship that he intended to come to expression in what Ephesians
5:32 terms "a great mystery," namely, the unbreakable covenantal
union between Christ and the church.

Every husband represents Christ in that marriage relationship.
So the question for *you* is whether you do that consciously and faithfully, or whether you defile him whom you represent.

Every wife represents the church in its relationship to Christ. Do
you do so faithfully? Do you live in that consciousness? Or are you
a picture of an apostate church?

The fact that God himself instituted marriage *as he did* is foundational to marriage. The divine institution of marriage, therefore,
is essential to living joyfully in marriage. It is the foundation upon
which marriage is established. When we talk about living joyfully
in marriage, we may look also at our consciousness of that divine
institution of marriage as being essential to securing the walls of joy
to that foundation.

Created by God

The institution of marriage was created by God. It is evident from
what God reveals to us in Scripture, beginning in Genesis 2, that
marriage is not merely something instituted by men or by govern-
ments to maintain respectability and safety in society.

God himself instituted marriage, doing so for a purpose. For
one thing, in mercy God has purposed that holy marriage reflect the
unbreakable relationship between Christ and his bride, the church.
And the family, the Christian home, is the place where he is pleased
to prepare his children through believing parents to be kings and

queens, princes and princesses in his everlasting kingdom. So we read in Psalm 45.

Marriage therefore serves God's purpose in forming *his own family*, gathered to live in the fellowship of his covenantal life, and that forevermore.

While marriage itself is a temporary institution, that is, until death parts us and until God's church is finally and completely united as one, marriage was created as an ordinance for all history. Far from being merely a human institution that may be used or ignored at whim, marriage was created and established by God himself, never to be redefined or shaped by human impulse or desires. That people attempt to do so is evident. That has been the case throughout history to one degree or another. But as the Scriptures cannot be broken, neither can the divine institution of marriage be dissolved by mere humans.

The ambivalence, the conflicting feelings toward marriage, that has many today holding this divine institution in contempt is understandable among those who reject God himself and the authority of his word. But such an attitude toward marriage may not be acceptable among Christians. Marriage is not just a legal piece of paper that provides certain legal protections. It is not a mere social institution that stifles "true love." It is a glorious institution created by the magnificent God of all glory, who seeks what is good for his people.

But we also have to realize that when so many in the world of our day have grown up in homes with father and mother at each other's throats, or homes where father and mother divorced and then remarried, thrusting the children into a combined family; where so many have grown up in homes without fathers and a husband-figure; and where the church has had no or little influence, it only stands to reason that multitudes have no conception of what a marriage ought to be.

We are quickly affected by faulty thinking when it comes to marriage. Just as in many other areas of the Christian life, we like to mark our own way. We like to make our own determinations as to what marriage is and involves. That begins with our sinful, self-seeking perspective of marriage as something that is for *my* benefit. As men, we might even point to Genesis 2 and find support for the idea of marriage being something to serve *me*, and more particularly for a wife being there simply *for me*.

So we must look more carefully at this institution of marriage and see what God did in giving man his wife, and what God expects from us concerning this relationship.

We must begin in Genesis 1:26–28, where we read God's conversation of fellowship within his own triune covenantal being, as he discusses man's creation:

26. And God said, Let us make man in our image, after our likeness: and let them have dominion over the fish of the sea, and over the fowl of the air, and over the cattle, and over all the earth, and over every creeping thing that creepeth upon the earth.

27. So God created man in his own image, in the image of God created he him; male and female created he them.

28. And God blessed them, and God said unto them, Be fruitful, and multiply, and replenish the earth, and subdue it: and have dominion over the fish of the sea, and over the fowl of the air, and over every living thing that moveth upon the earth.

He gave that calling to Adam and Eve, male and female.

But now in Genesis 2, where we have what might be called from a certain perspective "commentary" on chapter 1, we learn that male and female were not created at the same moment and in the same way. Man was first formed by a twofold act of God: "And the LORD

God formed man of the dust of the ground, and breathed into his nostrils the breath of life; and man became a living soul" (Gen. 2:7).

For a very brief period in the day that man was created, Adam lived alone. God created him a perfect being; and yet he was alone. There are many single men who feel alone. But we cannot really imagine what it was for Adam to be alone in that state of perfection. Though he had fellowship with God, Adam had no *human* companion, no companion of his own likeness with whom he could communicate.

Even in singleness we are never alone. The Bible says, "God setteth the solitary in families" (Ps. 68:6). He places his unmarried children in various congregations, in church families, to give them a special place so that they are not alone. They are *married*. As members of Christ's bride, they are married to Christ and thus are part of God's family. Not only those who are single but the congregation must understand that and the calling implied in that.

But Adam was *alone*. Not only that, but in the brief time—just a few hours apparently—that he was alone, Adam carried out the work that God had given him. He exercised dominion in the creation, caring for and naming the animals. As we read in Genesis 2:19, God brought the beasts and birds to Adam, to see what he would call them. God brought those creatures to Adam with *purpose*. For this follows what we read in verse 18: "And the LORD God said, It is not good that the man should be alone." As God brought those living creatures to Adam, Adam noticed that for each animal there was a mate.

Even though God had made man in his own image, after his own likeness, even though man was a perfect, sinless being, as a man he was incomplete. He was incomplete because he was alone, separated from something that he needed. Man was not created in the image of God in the sense of being a triune being. Man was not created with a tripersonal being, where he could have fellowship within himself and where he could radiate the love of God within himself as a human being. He was only one person, alone.

God brought the animals to Adam in order that Adam might see that in his own life there was a lack. "And Adam gave names to all cattle, and to the fowl of the air, and to every beast of the field; but for Adam there was not found an help meet for him" (Gen. 2:20).

Because God knew that it was not good that Adam be alone and because he had a higher purpose for Adam, he said, "I will make him an help *meet* for him," a counterpart for him (Gen. 2:18, emphasis added). God did not say, "I will make an equal to him." Understand now, I am talking about role, about function, not about dignity and value or lack of equality as a participant of salvation. As recipients and partakers of the wonder of salvation in Christ Jesus, male and female are one and equal (Gal. 3:28). But God did not say, "I will make an equal to the man"; certainly not, "I will make a competitor or rival opposite him." God said, "I will make him an help meet for him."

This phrase is often misunderstood. That is evident when people call wives "helpmeets," making one word out of what are two separate words. The woman was created a help meet for the man, that is, a help exactly fitted to him and his need. The idea is that the woman stands face to face with Adam, answering to his needs. We might say that God declares, "I will make an echo." The voice is Adam's need; the echo is what Eve will be. Isn't that beautiful? That is what God says. "I will make Adam an help answering to him."

So, speaking figuratively now, whatever goes out from Adam as the voice of his need is echoed perfectly by Eve's answer to that need.

Even children can understand this. They know what an echo is. There are some places you can go, especially in certain mountain ranges, but even in some buildings, where you can say something and what you say will be echoed back to you. "Hello...hello ...hello..." "Where are you...where are you...where are you..." Every little inflection in your voice, whether you speak high or low, loudly or softly, comes back in that echo, answering to your own voice.

Now God says, "I will make an help answering to Adam." Whatever Adam's needs are—physically, mentally, emotionally, as well as spiritually—Eve will be the complement. She will be just what man needs to fill the void, the lack, in his own life.

That this interpretation is indeed true is emphasized in the New Testament in 1 Corinthians 11, where the apostle Paul develops the truth of the man's headship over the woman. He gives the reason for this headship in verse 8, when he writes, "For the man is not of the woman: but the woman of the man." God did not take a rib from the woman and create a man. But God took a rib from Adam and from that rib formed the woman.

You realize that when you take this position and humbly receive God at his word, there are those who will say to you, "You don't really believe that ridiculous story, do you?!" Yes, I do. And it is not because God needed a rib to form a woman. He could have spoken and she would have been standing next to Adam. After all, he spoke galaxies into being by the sheer power of his word, we read in Psalm 33. But he used a rib from Adam because he would teach us something. That which he would teach us is spoken by the inspired apostle Paul in 1 Corinthians 11:9: "Neither was the man created for the woman; but the woman for the man." She was created out of the man to show both how inseparably connected is her life to the man's and that she was made for the man.

A Defined Relationship

Thus, marriage is a relationship not only instituted but *defined* by God.

I know very well what kind of reaction this gets among the liberated and ungodly women of various worldly organizations today. They rage with the charge that we deny the dignity of the woman.

The problem is, they cannot see that the truth set forth in Genesis 2 and the God-given place of the woman *is* her dignity.

This is the *glory* of the woman. Think of it. The perfectly created man, who was made from God's own hand, was incomplete until God made a woman for him. So important is that woman! Adam could say with rejoicing, "God made a woman for me! This is now bone of my bones and flesh of my flesh!" But at the same time, this truth is very humbling. While this is not the case today with all those who are single—again, because God has established his church for relationships and for helps to those who are unmarried—nevertheless, we men to whom God has given wives must recognize how important is that wife. I, as a man, was incomplete without God's provision in my wife. It is my glory, on the one hand, that God would think enough of me to make a help answering to my need. But at the same time, that is my humiliation, because I am not complete without her.

None but the woman could fill that need in Adam. That is the glory of her role and place. Recognizing that, Adam would treat her as *one* with him, a *part* of him—not separate from him, an object to use; but one with him.

So God brought together the one man and one woman in the bond of marriage.

Marriage's institution is strictly of God—one woman for one man. Again, *God* established that. We have here the origin of marriage. It is not a human institution. It is not subject to change to accommodate homosexuality or polyamory. We read in Genesis 2:22, "The LORD God...brought her unto the man." That was the first wedding ceremony. God instituted it. Adam himself had nothing to do with it. It was not that he decided he wanted to live with a woman and needed God's approval. Love did not come first, followed by the institution of marriage. Adam did not even know that marriage would be good for him until God revealed it to him.

This has clear implications for our lives today. If marriage is indeed a manmade institution, man may also do with that institution what he pleases. If he wants to put his wife aside for a younger woman, then he may divorce and remarry. He may abolish marriage altogether, which is exactly what many people are doing today. If marriage is only a *human* ordinance, there is nothing holy about it. Then what is being taught in public schools and at health clinics is not objectionable. It is simply a practical handling of social problems. If marriage were only a human institution, then humans would have every right to change it, even to include homosexual relationships. But all these corruptions of holy marriage are damnable when we understand that marriage is a holy ordinance of God. Human beings have no right to redefine the institution of marriage. Marriage is a divine institution, a creation ordinance established by God himself. For that reason, our understanding of marriage must be thoroughly biblical and filled with reverence for God who instituted it. And when we honor holy marriage, we do so recognizing it as a high calling and a blessed privilege given us by God.

So high is this calling of holy marriage that God has established it as the reflection of the relationship between Christ and his bride, the church. So Paul interprets this marriage ordinance in Genesis 2 when he writes in Ephesians 5:31–32, "For this cause shall a man leave his father and mother, and shall be joined unto his wife, and they two shall be one flesh. This is a great mystery: but I speak concerning Christ and the church."

This means that for us, who live after the fall into sin devastated the marriage relationship, the power of Christ's redemption has also embraced *this* relationship, restoring and renewing it and giving it to be, once again, the joyful relationship that God intended for marriage—in the way of obedience to him.

The Establishment of a Home

We learn from the text that marriage's divine institution is the establishment of a home. The glory of the "home life" of the covenantal God, the beauty of God's family established in Jesus Christ and his bride, is reflected in the marriage instituted by God in the beginning of his creation.

"Therefore shall a man leave his father and his mother," we read in Genesis 2:24. Here is revealed how marriage will be seen in the future. Adam and Eve had no father and mother to leave. Their children would. The emphasis here, therefore, is on the fact that marriage is the establishment of a home. Because God has so instituted holy marriage as good for man, a man shall leave his father and his mother to marry. By implication, the same holds true for the wife.

This element is most important, as is emphasized by its place in the text. This aspect of the marriage ordinance shows that the relationship of marriage is to take precedence over every other relationship, including the closest bond of the blood relationship. When you are married, your husband or your wife is to be first in your life under God. Together you establish a home that reflects the very covenantal life of God himself revealed in Christ and his bride.

The relationship in which a child stands to his or her parents is changed, therefore, when that child enters marriage.

When you marry, you are to leave the government of your parents. God has vested in your new relationship a new seat of government with the husband as the head. With that new seat of government, you understand, there comes the responsibility of decisionmaking. Parents are to honor that new relationship too, and not interfere.

We are also to leave father and mother emotionally. This is not to reject our calling to honor our parents. But your focus as a husband is to be your wife; and your focus as a wife is to be your husband. An uncut umbilical cord to a mother or father will bring great misery and invoke the fiercest hostility in the marriage relationship. If a newly married son or daughter continues to cling to his or her parents, calling every day and so on, the parents must put a stop to it, reminding their son or daughter of the calling of God to devote undivided attention to his or her new spouse. God commands us in marriage to leave father and mother, in order also that we might cleave unto our spouse.

Implied here as well is the fact that the marriage relationship is to take precedence over all other relationships.

If God mentions the closest tie, he necessarily includes the lesser ties. Sometimes before marriage young people build relationships that for one reason or another do not work out. Though one side or the other may have a strong desire for marriage, the desire is not mutual and the relationship is broken off. The young man or young woman who has suffered that pain must be careful that, before entering marriage with another, that former relationship is set aside. That also is implied in this necessary leaving of a former relationship in order to cleave to one husband or one wife in marriage.

The marriage relationship must also have precedence over the parent-child relationship. This also is an area where warnings to husbands and wives are not at all out of place. This warning is often most necessary for the wife. When the Lord blesses a marriage with children, it is the mother who bears the greatest responsibility in the day-to-day nurturing and care of the child. The time spent with the children is usually greater than the time spent with the husband. In the midst of our family life, we must be careful that our marriage relationships and fellowship as married couples is continually nurtured.

It is not that Scripture sets family life and marriage at odds. But there is here the establishment of priority. That is also for the sake of the children. Children must see the love of Christ exercised by their parents within their marriage relationship. When a husband or wife allows the child to slip between that intimate relationship of a married couple, he or she invites disastrous consequences to his or her disobedience to God's will. So a man shall leave his father and his mother; likewise shall the woman.

This is the divine institution of marriage. Because God has designed and instituted marriage, we must make every effort to understand and to submit to his purposes in this relationship. We are not to ignore what God requires of us in *any* aspect of our lives, also our marriages.

Chapter 3

A "One-Flesh" Relationship

Therefore shall a man leave his father and his mother, and shall cleave unto his wife: and they shall be one flesh.—Genesis 2:24

4. And he answered and said unto them, Have ye not read, that he which made them at the beginning made them male and female,

5. And said, For this cause shall a man leave father and mother, and shall cleave to his wife: and they twain shall be one flesh?

6. Wherefore they are no more twain, but one flesh. What therefore God hath joined together, let not man put asunder. —Matthew 19:4–6

Belonging to the divine institution of marriage is the fact that marriage is a one-flesh relationship. That is the second truth constituting an essential to a joyful marriage.

The relationship instituted by God himself in marriage is a reflection of the one-flesh relationship of Christ and his church. Let's not lose sight of that. Also our singles—those bereaved, those who have been forsaken, as well as those unmarried—*are yet married*.

Every one of us who belong to Jesus Christ by a living faith is married to *him*. That is foundational to a life of joy in whatever state we are. If you will experience joy in your life as a single, you will experience that joy only in the consciousness of your relationship to Jesus Christ, who loves you as more than a spouse. Remember what the apostle John wrote under the inspiration of the Holy Spirit in 1 John 1:3: "That which we have seen and heard declare we unto you, that ye also may have fellowship with us: and truly our fellowship is with the Father, and with his Son Jesus Christ." That is *the* marriage relationship God has established with us in Christ! The inspired apostle then followed those words with this: "And these things write we unto you, that your joy may be full" (v. 4).

Living in the consciousness of being one with Christ—that is the way of living joyfully, also in the marriage relationship. That blessedness of union with Christ comes to precious expression in the one-flesh relationship of holy marriage.

What a "One-Flesh" Relationship Is

What is meant by marriage being a one-flesh relationship? "Therefore shall a man leave his father and his mother, and shall cleave unto his wife: and they shall be one flesh" (Gen. 2:24).

Jesus reaffirmed that divine institution of marriage when he said in Matthew 19:6, "Wherefore they are no more twain, but one flesh. What therefore God hath *joined together*, let not man put asunder" (emphasis added). Notice, that concept "one flesh" is explained in part by Jesus when he speaks of what God has *joined together*. One flesh—a joining together.

That a man and a woman become one flesh certainly refers, in part, to the sexual aspect of marriage, what may be reverently referred to as "the act of marriage." That act is the God-given expression of the unique intimacy and union of marriage. There is to be found nothing dirty in the intimacy of the sexual union within holy marriage. We must not corrupt that holy union by taking a worldly and hedonistic perspective of it. Nor must we let the corruption of the ungodly cause us to view the sexual relationship as shameful when kept within the sanctity and intimacy of holy marriage. Even our children, as they come to maturity, need to understand that. We read in Hebrews 13:4, "Marriage is honourable in all, and the bed undefiled: but whoremongers and adulterers God will judge."

But there is more to be found in the expression "they two became one flesh." Besides the physical intimacy, the husband and wife who were formerly two become one flesh in every sense of the word. They are of one mind, having the mind of Christ. They are one in purpose, to serve the Lord their God. They are one in faith, one in hope, one in love. They enjoy each other's fellowship. They converse together, encourage each other, and provide spiritual support for each other on the pathway of life God gives them.

Though each having different roles and callings, they are not two, but one. Together the godly husband and wife are one flesh. Do you find it so in your own marriage? This is God's ordinance: "Therefore shall a man leave his father and his mother, and shall cleave unto his wife: and they shall be one flesh" (Gen. 2:24).

As this truth is also interpreted in the last part of Ephesians 5, let's not overlook the fact that the one-flesh relationship of marriage was established by God to display the intimacy and unbreakable union between Christ and his bride. Our Lord Jesus Christ left his Father to take the church as his bride. He sacrificially gave himself to take his bride into such an unbreakable union that he formed her a new creature in him. In the language of 1 Corinthians 6:17, "He that is joined unto the Lord is one spirit."

The oneness of marriage therefore is not just an empty shell. There is a complete intermingling of body and soul, an intimacy unmatched in any other earthly relationship.

So true, so intimate, is that one-flesh relationship that I have often described it in terms of a loaf of bread. God takes the ingredients of one man and one woman, with everything that has made each one the person that he or she is. He takes the genetic makeup of two individuals, he takes every experience of their lives from infancy to the moment of marriage. He takes their own experiences and many conversations as a couple prior to marriage. And on that wedding day, when they are declared husband and wife, God, as it were, takes those ingredients in those two individuals, not only mixing them, but baking them into one loaf. You realize that once you have mixed together the ingredients that make up that loaf of bread and bake it, you are never again going to be able to separate those ingredients. They have become one loaf. That is marriage. No one, and no legal action of divorce, can break that bond. It is impossible! "He that is joined unto the Lord is one spirit." That is what marriage represents.

Those who are single must realize that this is a description of the Christian life—the unbreakable union between us and Christ. We so foolishly try to break that union sometimes. Every time we sin, we commit spiritual adultery against Christ. But he is faithful. So faithful, as reflected in the marriage relationship, that when he takes a husband or wife through death, *he* breaks that marriage bond to take that person whom he loves into the perfect glory of the *true* marriage. But in doing so, he also reminds the spouse who remains just how real that one-flesh relationship is.

How It Is Expressed

Both Genesis 2:25 and Matthew 19:5 tell us just *how* that one-flesh relationship is expressed. Adam is to cleave to his wife. The apostle Peter explains that in part when he writes in 1 Peter 3:7, "Likewise, ye husbands, *dwell with* them according to knowledge, giving honour unto the wife, as unto the weaker vessel, and as being heirs together of the grace of life; that your prayers be not hindered" (emphasis added).

To cleave to her is to dwell with her. Paul gives the same calling, even when that spouse is unbelieving. There must be a dwelling together, not a separation or pulling away from. To confirm that this is the calling not only of the husband, but also of the wife, the same duty is given her in Psalm 45:10—"forget also thine own people, and thy father's house"—in order that she might cleave to her husband-king, the application of which is to the church as the bride of Christ. We are to dwell together, not forsaking each other's fellowship. We are to dwell together in order to carry out our callings within the holy bond of marriage. The likeness in our lives as Christians is the calling to separate from the world, in order to devote ourselves to our union with Christ. "You cannot serve God and mammon" (Matt. 6:24).

But notice as well from 1 Peter 3:7, husbands are to dwell with their wives "according to knowledge." That tells us yet more about how this one-flesh relationship is to be expressed. If you are a husband, you are to cleave to your wife as the lofty creature whom God has given you. Just as you cannot cleave to God without knowing him, you cannot cleave to your wife without knowing her. That takes ongoing interaction, careful attentiveness. You are to cleave to her, recognizing that she is a glorious creature, shaped by the very hands of God.

You realize that the woman historically has been trampled upon. By those who reject God's word, the woman has been badly treated through the years, used as little more than an object for enjoyment and as an ox to bear the yoke of labor in the home. Such treatment has contributed in large measure to her rebellion and rejection of man's headship. Even in the church, this evil treatment of the woman is sometimes seen with men who corrupt the biblical idea of headship and twist it to dictatorship. In the idolatry of self, they would look upon the woman as nothing more than their servant.

But such a corrupt idea and evil treatment of the woman is condemned simply by the account of the woman's creation in such a high place of honor, and by the command God gave Adam to cleave to his wife. It is biblical Christianity that restores woman to her lofty office in God's creation.

But there is more to be said about what it means to cleave to one's wife. The word "cleave" means "to be joined fast unto." The reference is not merely to the sexual aspect of marriage, as beautiful as that is within that holy bond, but this cleaving refers to a covenantal commitment before the face of God, a commitment in every aspect of life for the entirety of this earthly bond.

God ordained that marriage be intimate fellowship and communion between husband and wife. He instituted our marriages so that we two share our lives together, conversing with one another, sharing our burdens together, laughing together, and occasionally weeping together. Our covenantal fellowship with God is to be a walk with God *together* as husband and wife.

The apostle emphasizes the same thing in Ephesians 5, shedding upon this ordinance the light of the gospel, when he says to us husbands, "In your relationship with your wife, you are to be like Christ." And what does Christ do to his church? Paul uses two very tender words: he "nourishes" her and "cherishes" her. That is how you are to cleave to your wife—nourishing and cherishing her, being sensitive to her spiritual, intellectual, emotional, and physical needs. You are to be her *companion*, her most intimate friend.

How are you going to do that if you come home at night only to eat supper and sit down in front of the television to watch ball games or to play video games? How are you going to cleave to your wife, with *knowledge*, when you do not give her time for conversation, when you do not express your affectionate care for what she does for you, when you hardly have any social interaction with her?

There is a steep price to pay when a man ignores his wife. For most of us, this word heard anew must bring us to our knees in repentance before God and before our wives. Specifically, we must confess our sins of the idolatry of self. But where we have failed, we are called to conversion. And conversion, you understand, is beyond us. We must draw near to Christ. Only in Christ shall we, who are fallen, confess our sins and walk in obedience to this unchangeable ordinance of God.

Though this calling is given to the man, in the same way the woman is to cleave to her husband. I will not repeat that calling here, having already set it forth in her creation as the help meet for the man. Belonging also to that service as a help for your husband is that you as a wife are to be your husband's closest companion and friend.

The Source of This Intimacy

The source of this intimacy of the one-flesh relationship is the truth of God himself. We may not separate our theology, that is, our doctrine of God, from what our marriages must be. Any antipathy toward God's doctrine is devastating to marriage, for it is only in understanding God and his truth that we can understand marriage and the intimacy of the one-flesh relationship.

If you are married and want to live joyfully in that relationship, and if you are a member of Christ's bride and desire to flourish in the joy of his fellowship, then you must stand before the glory of God more and more.

To fail to stand before God is to make the intimacy of marriage merely a biological or social urge, an animal instinct. It is to fail to recognize the glory in which God created the one-flesh relationship. Our need for intimacy, for a one-flesh relationship—and let's remember again, marriage is the picture of what we *all* must enjoy with our intimate relationship to Jesus Christ—that need comes from our very creation in the image of God.

The fact that God has revealed himself as triune, three persons in one divine being, is the revelation of himself as the *covenantal*

God, the covenant being defined as the relationship of fellowship and love within the very life of God himself. Our God is the God of *relationships*. That is what sets him apart from all the gods of men's imaginations.

The reflection of this must also set apart our marriages. He is love, John tells us in his first epistle. That does not refer to the fact that God expresses that love outside himself. He *is* love. He is that within his own divine life. His own relationship is defined by love, by fellowship, by seeking his own glory in each of the three persons of the Godhead. We have seen this already in Genesis 1:26, where we took note of the fact that God had a conversation within his own divine being concerning man's creation.

God calls us to stand on holy ground and to observe something about his own covenantal life—the intimacy, the conversation, the fellowship, the three being united in will, in purpose, and in activity. And then we are told, "So God created man in his own image, in the image of God created he him; male and female created he them" (Gen. 1:27).

So important is that truth for our own understanding of who we are that God emphasizes it twice in Genesis 1:27: "So God created man in his own image, in the image of God created he him." Male and female individually, but emphatically together, reveal the image of God, his own covenantal life.

We were created for fellowship, for intimacy. As the Son of God would say, "I and my Father are one" (John 10:30), expressing the unity of his relationship to the Father through the Spirit. God has determined that our marriages express that unity in a one-flesh relationship.

Once again, it is important that also the unmarried remember that God has determined that *all* we as Christians express that unity found in his own covenantal life in our one-flesh relationship as Christ's bride to our exalted bridegroom. Our relationships therefore, whether in married life or in our life within God's church, are to glorify God in and through our relationship to Jesus Christ.

That is why we cannot fathom the depths of our human relationships until we begin to comprehend the depths of our union with Christ.

With eyes fixed upon Christ, we view marriage highly. God is glorified in this bond between a godly man and a godly woman.

Marriage must be a matter of prayer for our young people, and the calling and responsibilities of marriage a matter of serious Bible study. Our young men and young women must seek God's will in harmony with his word. For some, God's answer may not be the provision of a husband or wife. Though marriage is clearly the norm, it is not something for every man or woman. God has selected a number of his saints to live as single, occupying a particular and special place in his kingdom. But for those who walk in his ways and who find it his will that he provides you a godly husband or godly wife, you will find that the way of obedience to God in that relationship is a way of great joy and rich blessings.

If you have had the sorrow of growing up in a home where the marriage of your parents was not what it ought to have been, do not be lazy and repeat the same sinful behavior. We cannot express the one-flesh relationship of marriage without knowing and living in the fellowship of our Redeemer. To the extent that we grow by faith in that fellowship with Christ our bridegroom and bring that to expression in our own lives, to that extent we shall live joyfully in marriage and in our life in the midst of the congregation.

The truth of God is the source of our happiness also in marriage. My marriage is a manifestation of my theology. The consciousness of God's covenant and my place in that covenant makes my embrace of my wife the expression of my embrace of God. We must live in that knowledge.

Chapter 4

A BROKEN HOME

5. For God doth know that in the day ye eat thereof, then your eyes shall be opened, and ye shall be as gods, knowing good and evil.
6. And when the woman saw that the tree was good for food, and that it was pleasant to the eyes, and a tree to be desired to make one wise, she took of the fruit thereof, and did eat, and gave also unto her husband with her; and he did eat.
7. And the eyes of them both were opened, and they knew that they were naked; and they sewed fig leaves together, and made themselves aprons.—Genesis 3:5–7

When we consider the main theme of "Living Joyfully in Marriage," we must know that there are particular truths critical to understand if the bands of joy are to be fastened to relationships God has given us in marriage or to our relationships as members of Christ's bride to our Lord Jesus Christ.

First, we need to understand that God has divinely instituted marriage. That is not to be a mere platitude for us. We need to understand the significance of that wonder in all its application to us. What God has instituted, he has instituted for our good, not to make us feel miserable. But in that institution he has also established our *callings* within that union, requiring obedience, demanding that we uphold every aspect of that which he himself has instituted.

Second, we have considered the one-flesh relationship that defines marriage. God has given marriage to reflect the mystery that is the glorious, unbreakable relationship between Christ and his church. From that point of view, what God teaches us in marriage is applicable to everyone who is a member of Christ's bride, married or unmarried. If we will experience joy in our lives, whether within the bond of marriage or within Christ's church, we must live more and more in the consciousness of God's covenant with us in our Lord Jesus Christ and what the wonder of that relationship means to us.

A third element that belongs as an essential to a joyful marriage is the realization of the effect that sin has had upon this relationship.

We must come to grips with the reality of sin as it affects this relationship. Specifically, we must understand how the fall has affected us *personally*, but not to excuse our sinful behavior—for then we perish. We must understand how the fall has affected us personally in order that we might flee for refuge to the cross of Jesus Christ, confessing our sins both before God and before our spouses, there to find the wonderful redemption Christ has brought also to marriage, to *our* marriages. This understanding is important so that the wonder of our redemption be applied by us in lives of thankful obedience to his word.

Marriage was given for the purpose of revealing the blessedness of covenantal fellowship as the revelation of God's own glorious covenantal life. The reason God gave Adam his wife was that she might help him in his service of God. Adam's calling was also to glorify God in his care for his wife. This is something our young adults have to remember and our children have to be taught.

Marriage was not just given for our self-satisfaction and our own personal happiness. God gave marriage for his own glory, to reveal to his creatures, Adam and Eve, what God's own covenantal life means in its earthly application. That is why, as we have seen, to consider marriage is to consider a truth about God that is just as important for those who are *not* married. God ordained the state of marriage to teach us about our relationship to God through Jesus Christ. That is evident in the second chapter of Hosea's prophecy, Hosea 2:19–20, where Jehovah says to his church, "And I will betroth thee unto me for ever; yea, I will betroth thee unto me in righteousness, and in judgment, and in lovingkindness, and in mercies. I will even betroth thee unto me in faithfulness: and thou shalt know the LORD."

But in Genesis 3:5–7 we find the devastating consequences that the fall into sin had upon the marriage relationship. Here we consider particularly the effects of the fall upon the marriage of Adam and Eve.

The Devastation of the Fall

The entire context of Genesis 3, and particularly verses 5–7, sets forth the fall of our first parents, Adam and Eve, and the devastating effects of that fall into sin.

It should go without saying, but unfortunately must be said in our day when so much of the church has come under the influence of evolutionary theory, that we have♠ this text a historical account that explains why the world is filled with so many sorrows, so much strife, and such a multitude of evils, as is our own sad experience.

This is not myth. It is not allegory. It is not a mere story. This is the biblical, historical record of sin's entrance into the world, and therefore the entrance of death into the world.

This explains why the marriage form that historically has been used in marriage ceremonies in Reformed churches begins with stark realism: "Whereas married persons are generally, by reason of sin, subject to many troubles and afflictions."[1]

The reality of all the troubles we experience is found at its root

---

1 Form for the Confirmation of Marriage before the Church, in *The Confessions and the Church Order of the Protestant Reformed Churches* (Grandville, MI: Protestant Reformed Churches in America, 2005), 306.

in Genesis 3. And the historical reality of what is recorded here is confirmed by several New Testament passages, all of which point back to a real Adam, the first man, and Eve his wife, the first woman, who were tempted by Satan appearing in a serpent to deceive Eve and to bring about the downfall of the entire human race that would follow. Every New Testament passage that refers back to this reality speaks of this historical event as the way in which sin entered the world, and death by sin.

Genesis 3 therefore is monumental to our understanding of the world in which we live, the sorrows that we endure, and the difficulties we experience in relationships, as well as the guilt and sin from which we must be delivered. Everything concerning our understanding of man, of relationships, of suffering and death, rests on this foundation of the historical account of the fall of our first parents.

Instrumental in this devastating fall of Adam and Eve was the lie of Satan, calling into question God's character, first, and then insisting that his word is not true. "Ye shall not surely die: for God doth know that in the day ye eat thereof, then your eyes shall be opened, and ye shall be as gods, knowing good and evil" (Gen. 3:4–5).

Here sin is revealed in its deepest principle, to deny God's sovereignty and to usurp the authority of his word. Satan, whose very name means "adversary," shows himself as the liar, the devil, that he is. He would convince Eve, as always he is attempting to convince us, that he has her well-being in mind, that he has *our* well-being in mind—and God does not. "You know better than *God*," he whispers in our ears.

Eve fell for it. Now we do too. It does not take much, either, for us to forget all about God's way. Thinking more highly of ourselves than we ought to think, we are quite confident that we know best and can do things quite well ourselves, thank you very much! That attitude comes to clear expression as we live our lives without seeking to bring our thoughts and actions into conformity to the word of God, to his will.

It is not my purpose here to unfold the account of the temptation and fall. I call your attention rather to the devastating effects of that fall, also as applied to the relationship between Adam and Eve.

But there is one element of the temptation that is connected with that relationship of Adam and Eve. I refer to the fact that Satan did not approach Adam, but the woman, by means of the serpent. If we ask why that was, the answer would be found in what we have seen in 1 Peter 3:7. There, you remember, we heard the call given to husbands to dwell with their wives according to knowledge, giving honor to them "as unto the weaker vessel."

There was a weakness that the devil himself observed in the woman. Understand well, that was *not* a moral or spiritual weakness. God created both man and woman perfect and in his own image. The weakness therefore refers to the *kind* of creature that God made her. Even as she was the provision for the particular needs of her husband, Eve was created different from the man in more than physical appearance. To know the needs of her husband and children, God gave her certain sensitivities, a tenderness and compassion fit for her role as a wife and mother. She was not created to be the provider, the defender, the leader, the protector. God created her a nurturer, perfectly fitting for her calling as a wife and mother. But those peculiar gifts as the weaker vessel would also be her greatest vulnerability.

Adam was given the calling to provide for his wife, to protect and defend her, and to lead her, in order that she might exercise her high calling in the role that God gave her. So important is it that the husband recognizes his calling to lead as the head, that the woman is explicitly told in 1 Timothy 2 that she is not to usurp authority over the man. Man is to exercise his calling even as Christ is the head of the church. So in 1 Corinthians 14:35 wives are told, "If they will learn any thing, let them ask their husbands at home." Again, this is not a matter of intellectual inferiority, for many wives have intellectual gifts superior to those of their husbands. This is a matter of the distinct roles and callings God has given male and female and the natures with which he created them for those callings.

Thus when we look at the account of the fall, and see how Satan approached the woman, we may understand that immediately he would attack marriage, and that by attempting to get the weaker vessel to deny the headship of the man.

The devastation of the fall, however, is especially seen in the tearing apart of relationships.

Immediately upon partaking of the forbidden fruit of the tree of knowledge of good and evil, the woman experienced a change that brought complete separation spiritually, not only from God, but also from her husband. By listening and succumbing to the devil's lie, she decided that God cannot be trusted and that his rules are oppressive. She decided that God was not looking out for her good; he was simply restricting her from joy and pleasure. She said to herself, "If I really want to enjoy life, I'm the one to decide how to do that. I need to be free! I need to grow, to express myself. To be *restricted*, how can *that* be for my good? I ought to be free to do as I please!" That's a common argument even today, isn't it? "My body, my choice" is not only the motto of the pro-abortion movement, but an expression that conveys the thinking of all human beings who have rejected God and his authoritative word.

Eve had already fallen when those thoughts entered her mind. When she began to think that Satan was right, she had already fallen. She had impugned God's motives, called into question his character, and rejected his word. Lust arose in her heart. James 1:15 tells us that "when lust hath conceived, it bringeth forth sin." To reach up and pull off that beautiful piece of fruit was only the natural consequence of the sin that had entered her heart. You realize that if you were to have a relationship with someone, which relationship was established in perfect fellowship and love, a relationship of trust therefore, and suddenly you were to judge for ill that person's motives and no longer trust that person, you would no longer have a relationship with that person. Instantly there would be a breach.

Eve no longer had a relationship with her Creator. She no longer experienced the love for God that had been her life up to that moment. But it was really far worse. The reason the woman no longer loved God was because she had come under the wrath of God, the wrath that works death. The destruction of that relationship by the woman's fall meant that she now lived apart from God. And the Bible tells us in Psalm 73 that to live apart from God is death.

One thing we must never forget about God. He seeks his own glory in everything. He is jealous for his own glory. God has a right to be jealous. He alone is God. He alone created us. We are mere creatures, subject to him always, in everything. Moreover, he created us to serve him, to glorify him. If there is one thing God cannot tolerate, it is anybody who would pretend to be like him, who would pretend to be his equal.

Satan knows that. He tried it. You read about it in Isaiah 14:12–15. "I will be like the most High"! That is what he said. And instantly God cast him out of heaven.

But Satan does not like being alone. He would have us join him. He would have *you* join him. That is what the woman did. And immediately the jealousy of God was known in her heart. She felt his hot displeasure. She now knew evil. But she knew it as the destructive power that was consuming her from that moment. Her relationship with God had been destroyed, torn apart. No longer her friend-sovereign; he was now her enemy. That is what sin does—it tears apart relationships!

The same was true of her relationship to her husband. The destructive power of God's wrath that began consuming her instantly also made her acutely aware of the breach that had taken place between her and her husband. She no longer enjoyed the love toward her husband that had formed the joy of their relationship. Unrighteousness does not mix with holiness. Eve could not tolerate the fellowship of a sinless, holy husband. It was not a fit. They were no longer compatible.

It was not that Eve's appearance changed. She did not suddenly become a devil. She was as beautiful as ever—outwardly. Adam would have been just as attracted to her, not knowing how depraved her heart and nature had become. But spiritually they were no longer compatible. In order for their relationship to continue in any form, she would have to take him down to her level. So she immediately sought to entice him into the fellowship of her darkness. The text indicates that it did not take much at all for the woman to entice the man to walk the same path with her. For we simply read that she "gave also unto her husband with her; and he did eat" (Gen. 3:6).

The one whom God had given to Adam to help him on the pathway of life instead became his stumbling block, the one to drag him down into the pit of sin's devastation.

Does that make Adam less to blame? Interesting question, isn't it? It is a question that naturally arises in the minds of us who are always trying to shift the blame. But the Bible makes clear: because of Adam's place as head, *he* bears the responsibility. You can never get away from that, men. If you are a husband, you answer to God for everything that takes place in your home. That is your responsibility. That is why it is important that you lead your wife and family in the right way spiritually. "But I would have you know, that the head of every man is Christ; and the head of every woman is the man; and the head of Christ is God" (1 Cor. 11:3). That is the principle of headship that God maintains always. Husbands are responsible for the actions of their wives and children. But Eve brought Adam down because their relationship had been destroyed.

The devastating effect of the fall, the tearing apart of relationships with both God and one another, also became manifest in a variety of ways.

The poisoning of that well of relationships was seen especially in this, that we became entirely self-centered. You can see that in the fall of the woman. Her choice was all about self. She made a choice that would advance her*self* above the mere state of a creature formed to serve God. God had created her to serve him. Belonging to that service of him would also be her service to her husband.

Now the focus is no longer on God, nor on what he requires of us in the relationship that he has established in marriage. The focus is on *self*. Eve fell into the idolatry of self. Adam's fall did the same. Ever since, there is something extremely seductive about the worship of self and our own desires. Especially if we are mistreated by a spouse, we are easily seduced to worship self and serve our own interests instead of exercising ourselves in self-sacrificial love, the love of giving for the welfare of the other.

The sad thing is, as revealed in verse 7, with that idolatry of self comes the opposite of what we seek. We would seek our own happiness in our own way. But instead of happiness comes guilt and shame.

The hurt brought into the relationship of Adam and Eve by their fall into sin is incalculable. With the separation from God and from each other came something painful, something that they had never experienced before. They became conscious of thoughts that they had never thought before. And they experienced shame. To such a degree did they experience shame that they tried to hide themselves from God and from each other. They took fig leaves and sewed them together to cover their loins. The very part of their bodies that gave them the most intimate expression of their fellowship, that which was a source of pure, untainted joy, was now an inescapable reminder of the breach of fellowship, the separation that now marred their relationship, the *loss* of pure joy. They saw even in their bodies the brokenness that their fall had brought into their home.

The Effects of Brokenness upon Us

This brokenness affects us. It affects our homes and our relationships deeply. The reason is found in our relationship to those first parents. Adam stood as the legal head of the whole human race that would come from him. He stood there by God's appointment. To go into this doctrine at length is not my purpose here. But Romans 5:12–21 tells us that because Adam was our legal head, when he fell, we fell with him. By his offense, God's judgment came upon us all to condemnation. That is to say, you and I are as guilty as Adam.

God has declared us guilty. Therefore, the punishment that we must bear is death—death, don't forget, not as you see it in the funeral home, made to look like peaceful sleep and covered with beautiful flowers. The death that we bear is that of a rotting stench that permeates everything we think and say and touch, death that comes to expression in a multitude of sins—also sins against each other.

We must understand how the devastation of the fall affects us in order to have a realistic view of marriage, of relationships, and of what it takes to see those relationships restored and made holy once again. If we are to experience the joy that ought to be ours in our marriages and in our place in Christ's church and in relationship with him, we must consciously come to grips with the sinfulness of our own sins within the marriage relationship—whether as husbands and wives or as members of Christ's bride in relationship to him.

Young people must understand that in the midst of premarital relationships, when you are trying to get to know another person spiritually, you also have to guard your own feelings and desires. Those warm and fuzzy feelings toward each other can make it very difficult even to *want* to take a hard and honest look at reality.

We often hear a relationship spoken of in terms of a "romance." Do you know what that word means? Listen to the dictionary definition of *romance*: "A fictitious tale of wonderful and extraordinary events, characterized by a non-realistic and idealizing use of the imagination."[2] If you want to make joyful marriage impossible to achieve, that is the way to do it.

You have to face reality, and you have to know what it takes for your marriage to be God-glorifying. If, before marriage, you are afraid to talk about issues that need to be discussed, because you are afraid that such discussion may disrupt the pleasantries of your relationship; if you are afraid to apply the light of God's truth to an area in which you might differ, because it will endanger your affections toward each other, you ought not to be married. You will never experience the true joy of a holy marriage if you are concealing things, refusing to deal with things, and failing to stand before God's word *together*. It will never work.

We need to stand before the stark reality of sin and see it for what it is.

Every element of dysfunction, of brokenness, of miscommunication; every biting word, every failure to express our love one for another, is rooted in sin.

Every act of selfishness belongs to the brokenness that our own sinfulness brings into our relationships. Every time we look at marriage, or any other relationship, as a matter of "what's in it for me?" instead of "what can I contribute to the strengthening of this relationship?" we bring to expression that idolatry of self that permeates our very natures since the fall.

This reality of sin is not something to be shrugged off. It may not be ignored. This is not how God would have us live. In marriage or in single life, God calls us to holiness, "without which no man shall see the Lord," we read in Hebrews 12:14.

We must know this in order to see our great need for marriage to be restored. Again, that is true for the marriages of husbands and

---

2 *Webster's New World College Dictionary*, 4th ed. (Foster City, CA: IDG Books Worldwide, Inc., 1999), s.v. "romance."

wives, but just as true for the real marriage of the church to Christ, and therefore for us as Christians in all the relationships within that bride of Christ.

Where there is a breach, there is sin that must be repented of. Where there is an attempt to hold one at arm's length, where there is rejection of a member of Christ's bride or of a spouse in the marriage relationship that reflects the relationship between Christ's bride and himself, there is an offense against God that, barring repentance, will bring devastation to the relationship and beyond as the fruit of God's wrathful judgment. There is no joy to be found in a broken home. Our homes therefore may not be left broken.

Our Only Hope

Our hope for the restoration of marriage and home life is found in the faithfulness of Jehovah to his covenant.

While we live within our own marriages with constant reminders of the devastating effects of sin, we must not lose sight of the fact that God's purpose in our marriages has not changed. We may never settle for less than what God requires of us, with the excuse that we are sinful. God never removes from us the high calling that he has given us. That calling, don't forget, is that we reflect his covenantal life and the perfect, unbreakable covenantal relationship between Christ and his church. When we remember that, we may never settle for less.

The chasm between the biblical view of marriage and how marriage is viewed in our culture has probably never been larger. To most, the biblical view of marriage is seen as ridiculous. We must not fall into that way of thinking.

If Jesus' own disciples had to be reminded of that, so do we. You remember, from Matthew 19, that when the Pharisees tried to trap Jesus into contradicting the law of Moses, one of the ways they did that was by putting him to the test concerning marriage, and particularly divorce. When Jesus upheld the original creation ordinance of God concerning marriage, his own disciples were astounded. It seemed to them as something absolutely impossible. In fact, they said, "If that's the standard, it's better that a man not marry!"

"But he said unto them, All men cannot receive this saying, save they to whom it is given" (Matt. 19:11). In other words, "While those who reject the authority of God's word and God's ordinance concerning marriage cannot receive this, this saying is given to *you*, who are mine." Implied is the fact that Christ has redeemed marriage, a wonder that reflects the redemption of his bride the church.

That means, with concrete application, that we cannot expect the magnificent purpose of God in marriage to be upheld in a world where the main religion is the idolatry of self, and the high point of doctrine is independence or self-determination. We cannot expect the beauty of marriage to be reflected in those who worship personal pleasure and entertainment, including uninhibited sexual gratification. When *our* lives are characterized by such idolatry, our marriages are going to be a mess. Worse, they are going to be a blasphemous portrayal of Christ and the church.

We need Christ.

We need Christ daily. We need him to cleanse us. We need him to sanctify us. We need him to fill us with the love necessary to live in the holiness to which he calls us—not only in our marriages, but as partakers of *the* marriage that is our relationship to him as his bride.

Do not think you can live without him. Do not think you can do marriage your own way. Do not think you can get by being a hearer of his word and not a doer. The consequences are devastating. Adam and Eve experienced it. So have we.

But you have been bought with a price—even the precious blood of our bridegroom, Jesus Christ. Second Corinthians 5:15 tells us that he died "that they which live should not henceforth live unto themselves, but unto him which died for them, and rose again." Live, therefore, as the new creature you are in Christ Jesus.

Chapter 5

MARRIAGE RESTORED

Unto Adam also and to his wife did the LORD God make coats of skins, and clothed them.—Genesis 3:21

We consider now the wonder of marriage's restoration. This restoration is a wonder of God's grace that reaches far beyond the marriage relationship. It is in fact the wonder of salvation! God would restore us into the joyful experience of his covenantal fellowship once again. But to do so would require the shedding of blood.

The Hopeless Situation

To Adam and Eve, the effects of their fall into sin were so palpable, and affected their relationship in every respect and to such a degree, that the restoration of what they had enjoyed before the fall appeared hopeless. That is evident even in the various aspects of the curse that God pronounced upon the woman and upon the man. Let's look at those briefly.

"Unto the woman he said, I will greatly multiply thy sorrow and thy conception; in sorrow thou shalt bring forth children; and thy desire shall be to thy husband, and he shall rule over thee" (Gen. 3:16).

There are several elements involved in that very real and ever-present consequence of the fall.

For one thing, and this regarding the consequences not only for Eve but for Adam as well, and for us their posterity, these are constant reminders that we have sinned against God. In the whole course of our earthly existence, we cannot escape the devastating effects of death. For the woman, even at the early stages of entering the years of childbearing, that involves the monthly cycle with its accompanying effects upon the body, physically and emotionally. It involves the particular infirmities that result from conception and carrying a child in the womb, as well as the suffering of childbirth itself.

But bringing forth children involves many more sorrows for the mother. Because of the fall, we can only bring forth children who bear the same effects of the fall and the same consequences of Adam's guilt. We are conceived and born in sin. We bring forth children who are spiritually stillborn, dead in trespasses and sins. Belonging to the sorrows of bringing forth children, therefore, is the fact that the mother has to deal with those sinful children all day every day. For the believing woman of God's covenant comes the blessed reminder of the gospel that her high calling bears wonderful fruit in and by Jesus Christ. Paul writes in 1 Timothy 2:15 that women are saved in childbearing. In the consciousness that God uses your labors to bring forth and gather his church and to establish his covenant in continued generations, you bring forth children and devote your life to nurturing and instructing them. But you do so facing many sorrows and even daily trials.

Compounding the difficulty for the woman was her now-defiled relationship to her husband. "Thy desire shall be to thy husband" (Gen. 3:16). That word "desire" means "to want" or "to pursue." The idea is that of following behind like a puppy. Probably the starkest display of this in the world is seen in the abused wife who covers up her husband's abuse.

I remember going into a home—not as a pastor but doing emergency medical work—where the police were on the scene of a woman who had been beaten so badly by her husband that we did not know if she would live. The only words you could understand from her were, "I won't press charges." That was during a very frustrating time for law enforcement, when the law required the one assaulted to press charges. Officers could not even arrest the husband without that wife agreeing to press charges. So they and we would see case after case of an abused wife showing the depths of her desire toward her husband. Today the laws have been changed so that the man who shoves his wife is subject to arrest for misdemeanor assault. The law now reflects a little more clearly the gross sin that a man commits in laying hands upon his wife. But that is just the starkest display of the woman's bondage to sin's consequences.

The devastating effects of the fall upon that glorious relationship are experienced in many sorrowful reminders of what was lost by listening to Satan.

Whereas the woman had made a conscious decision to usurp her husband's place as the head, and then to take him under her control, the result was a loss of the freedom and nurture that she had enjoyed in the fellowship of love with her husband. Now she is subject to that husband, who no longer stands in that beautiful relationship God originally established but rules over her in a way that reflects his own sinfulness. Which is to say, sometimes he will be a jerk. He will not help his wife; he will be demanding; he will act as if all he has to be concerned about is working to provide for the family. Everything else falls on the wife. He is going to abuse his headship. He is going to defile his headship. He is going to add to the sorrows of her life. And she has to be subject to him even when he does not deserve the help she gives him. The woman has to be subject to him because that is what *God* requires of her.

That is not to say she refuses to address her husband's sins. That is not to say she covers up his sins. That is not to say she does not use the law to protect herself, if necessary—and may God forbid that such wickedness be found among the husbands in the church. But in the normal everyday and sometimes difficult circumstances of living with her husband, she cannot escape the subjection to which God calls her.

The situation would appear just as hopeless for the man, in light of the consequences of his fall.

17. And unto Adam he said, Because thou hast hearkened unto the voice of thy wife, and hast eaten of the tree, of which I commanded thee, saying, Thou shalt not eat of it: cursed is the ground for thy sake; in sorrow shalt thou eat of it all the days of thy life;
18. Thorns also and thistles shall it bring forth to thee; and thou shalt eat the herb of the field;
19. In the sweat of thy face shalt thou eat bread, till thou return unto the ground; for out of it wast thou taken: for dust thou art, and unto dust shalt thou return. (Gen. 3:17–19)

The effects of the curse in the creation are manifold. We only consider a narrow application of those effects in this connection. How did that curse upon the creation affect man? To that question we find that death presses upon man on every side. The calling God had given him to subdue the creation, to be the provider and protector of his wife, has become a constant exercise in futility. We find our calling to be providers so difficult sometimes that we can neglect the other aspects of our callings as husbands.

We husbands forget that our chief calling in marriage is to love our wives, to nurture and cherish them as Christ does the church. We forget that the chief calling of a husband is to come to expression in his *headship* of his wife, a headship that is not tyranny. It is not an expression of headship that belittles the wife and degrades her and treats her like a child. It is not godly headship by which a husband would suppress his wife, using her as a footstool for his own exaltation. Godly headship comes to expression in that husband who leads, especially *spiritually*, and who reflects Christ as he leads his bride the church. We also can easily forget that belonging to the calling of a husband is that he *dwells with* his wife.

There are times in our lives when the effects of the fall dominate our own thinking and even our treatment of each other. There is a reason, after all, that the Holy Spirit addresses husbands in Colossians 3:19, "Husbands, love your wives, and be not bitter against them." There is a reason wives and mothers must be taught "to love their husbands, to love their children" (Titus 2:4). There are so many difficulties to face that we begin to let those difficulties shape our perspective. We let those stresses in life affect our relationships.

Perhaps you women, especially mothers, dealing with the frustrations of seeing the same sins coming to expression in your children day after day, begin to express that frustration in a sinful way, not only toward your children, but even toward your husband. After being bombarded with the running arguments of the children, perhaps you find yourself tuning out the noise. You are not listening as you must, in order to be able biblically to address the heart issues of your children's sins. But in tuning out your children, it can become an easy step also to tune out your husband. Perhaps seeing the sins of your husband, you begin to respond the same way. Whereas Proverbs 16:24 reminds us, "Pleasant words are as an honeycomb, sweet to the soul, and health to the bones," instead it is easy to be as those against whom Solomon warns us, who speak hastily, entering into contention and stirring up strife.

In addition, men all too often succumb to the effects of the fall and its influences upon our sinful pride. Perhaps you as a husband come home after a difficult day at work, to express your impatience and frustrations toward your wife and children. They did not have anything to do with the frustrations of the day, but you make them feel the brunt of it.

Again, every day we are confronted by the sights and sounds of a distressed creation and distressed relationships. These things have become such familiar background noise that we tend to block it out, even when those sights and sounds of distress are found coming from our own wives and children or fellow members of God's family, even our own church family. We become so self-centered that we no longer pay attention.

How many women complain that their husbands do not listen? And then husbands attempt to excuse it. In what appears to be the hopeless situation of the effects of the fall, we tell our wives that their expectations are unrealistic, that the problem is with them, not with us. (We have to attempt to maintain our authority, after all, don't we—let them know who is boss?)

But that is not the way God intended marriage to be. He did not establish that institution for *us* to shape according to our own foolishness. He maintains his righteousness in telling us what our marriages are to be. And he accepts nothing less.

For Adam and Eve, the situation was entirely hopeless—as it is for us and our marriages—except for one thing. God purposed to redeem us and to reconcile us unto himself. In doing so, he would maintain the covenantal relationship for which he created man, which covenantal relationship—let's not forget—would be reflected in the *marriage* relationship of husband and wife *and* of Christ and his bride.

By a wonder of his grace God would restore marriage!

The Powerful Cleansing

That could only be done by powerfully cleansing his people.

What fig leaves are we wearing? We have seen how Adam and Eve tried to hide themselves. God would teach them the folly of trying to flee from him and his word. It is impossible to live joyfully in marriage or as a Christian while trying to cover up our own sins and foolishness. To persist in the way of folly is destructive, robbing us even of the possibility of joy. God would teach Adam and Eve and us that there is nothing we can do to restore the joyfulness of his fellowship, also in our marriages. God will never be impressed with our futile offerings of personal achievements. They are empty to him, as empty as Adam's and Eve's fig leaves. We must see the wonder of God clothing them with coats of skins.

What does that mean?

For one thing, God is showing Adam and Eve that their self-made coverings would never do. Their covering could only come in the way of death. They would never again enjoy life and fellowship with God the way they had in the garden and at the tree of life. Nor could they ever enjoy that life and fellowship with God by bringing something to him. They had nothing to bring. They had no right to take of God's own creation and to bring a gift for which they could expect his favor. If they were to be cleansed from their guilt and shame, if they were to be restored to the consciousness of God's fellowship, God himself must provide what is necessary for their redemption.

So *he* provided a sacrifice and *he* made them partakers of that sacrifice. How was that provision of their clothing made? A coat of skin cannot be fashioned without the shedding of blood. A life had to be taken for them to escape their lives being taken. Another must suffer their punishment if they are to escape the punishment that their sins required. God sacrificed one of his own creatures. And from that creature he took the skin and clothed Adam and Eve.

We have to believe, in light of the promise of Genesis 3:15, that God explained to them that this was a type, the reality of which they had to lay hold of by faith. But can you imagine what it was like for them to be clothed in this way? It was not as if they had experience in tanning hides. It was not as if they had smelled death before. Those skins must have smelled vile. It is as if God said, "You proud man, who thought you could choose your own way; I will take the stinking skin of a beast as having more value than *anything* you can bring."

By that shedding of blood, God not only powerfully cleansed, but clothed our first parents with *righteousness*. He did that—even as he makes clear to us in his word—by the shedding of blood that pointed as a type to the shedding of *Christ's* blood, the Lamb of God who would take away the sin of world.

God taught his people that they must live by faith. He said, "The chasm between what you were and what you are now is infinite. You cannot possibly bridge it. You clothed yourselves in an attempt to cover yourselves. You need to be aware that your clothing is to serve as your own confession that you are not what you should be. You need to be clothed, but not only to confess your shame. You need to be clothed with righteousness."

We must embrace what God has done in his merciful redemption of us. By faith we must fix our eyes upon Jesus, the Lamb of God, whose righteousness alone has cleansed us and redeemed us from all our iniquities. In him is our restoration to the marriage covenant with God himself, as he embraces us again into the fellowship of his family life and love. But that also means that in Christ is the restoration of the marriages of his children, whose marriages *reflect* that most glorious relationship of Christ and the church.

The Amazing Implications

The implications are seen in the very nature of the sacrifice offered on our behalf and the work of God's grace in so clothing us.

Remember, the hopelessness into which marriage was cast by the fall into sin was hopelessness because of the inherent *selfishness* to which man and woman committed themselves.

As we have seen, in order to live joyfully in marriage, we must be delivered from that idolatry of self that would make it impossible for two to live as one. The wonder of the salvation that God gave Adam and Eve, and that he gives us in Christ Jesus, is that the very salvation of which we are partakers as husbands and wives has been given us *sacrificially*. Our salvation comes by self-sacrifice. The bridegroom of the church, our Lord Jesus Christ, gave himself to the death of the cross for us! He purchased us as his own bride by the shedding of his blood for us. That is what it took; that was the only price that could possibly make us fit to be his bride.

To enjoy the covenantal life and fellowship of the perfectly holy God, we had to be reconciled to him by the death of our bridegroom upon the cross. But that death, that self-denying sacrifice of love, also clothed us with the white robes of Christ's righteousness and made us bone of *his* bones and flesh of *his* flesh. That is what it is to be married to Christ! That is what it is to be a Christian! You—not just married couples now, but all our singles and our children too—you who are in Christ Jesus are *married*. You are married to him! That is the only way of putting off the idolatry of self. To put off the idolatry of self, and to give ourselves to the cause of our husband, Christ, is the way in which we live the Christian life joyfully.

That life of Christ in us has tremendous implications when it comes to marriage. It is by that life of Christ in us that living joyfully in marriage not only is possible but must be our *expectation*. We look for that life of Christ to be manifest in us. We labor by faith to bring that life of Christ to expression. That must be the case when Christ lives in us. He does not just take a seat in our heart by his Holy Spirit, there to dwell in silence. He *lives!* His life thrills our souls and comes to expression in the new creatures he has made of us.

In marriage, God works to deliver us from that ingrained sin of self-centeredness. He joins a man to a wife, and a woman to her husband. He takes two individuals who are very different—sinners too—and he points them to Christ. In our own spiritual battle because of our own sinfulness as well as that of our spouse, as we struggle to love and to lay aside our self-centeredness, God points us to the model marriage. He points us to Christ. In him we see what love is and how it is expressed. Love is not a mere feeling. It is an *act* of self-sacrificial giving, an act that seeks the good of its object. Love is an act of giving *unconditionally*, even when the spouse does not deserve it.

So we read in Ephesians 5:25–27:

25. Husbands, love your wives, even as Christ also loved the church, and gave himself for it;
26. That he might sanctify and cleanse it with the washing of water by the word,
27. That he might present it to himself a glorious church, not having spot, or wrinkle, or any such thing; but that it should be holy and without blemish.

That is *Christ's* word to men, a word that he also applies powerfully by his Holy Spirit in us, so that we bring it to practice—being not just hearers of the word, but doers also.

This same love, this same sacrificial giving, is required also of wives toward their husbands. I realize that the emphasis for the wives in Ephesians 5 is on the word "submit." But Titus 2:4 makes clear that wives also are called to love their husbands. This is not only what is *expected* of us; but these are the *blessings* of marriage restored by the power of God's love and grace in Christ Jesus.

This selflessness and self-sacrifice that flows from Christ's life in us and comes to expression in our marriages is seen as the opposite of that self-centeredness that belongs to our sinful natures and the fallen human perspective. The gospel of life in Christ Jesus transforms our thinking toward our spouses, esteems them better than ourselves (Phil. 2:3), removes the critical spirit, destroys the blame-shifting, dissolves the bitterness, and gives us to see the joy in this relationship that has been redeemed to reflect the mystery of Christ and the church.

This truth ties the decor of joy to the house of marriage. Living joyfully in marriage is the evidence of being clothed by the righteousness of Jesus Christ. Without *that* righteousness, no marriage can be right in God's sight. In that righteousness and living out of that life, marriage is seen and experienced as holy, magnificent, and a great blessing.

Chapter 6

ONLY IN THE LORD

Can two walk together, except they be agreed?—Amos 3:3

...only in the Lord.—1 Corinthians 7:39

When you read from Genesis 24:1–9 and Deuteronomy 7:1–11, and then look at Amos 3:3 and the closing words of 1 Corinthians 7:39, you find that these four passages all have in common the necessary spiritual unity for a healthy marriage relationship.

Belonging to the essentials of that which girds a marriage with joy is a necessary unity between husband and wife, a spiritual unity that reflects the holiness of God himself and the unity of his own covenantal relationship.

Apart from that unity, the joy that God would have our marriages reflect is an impossibility. Such joy is an impossibility because a marriage where there is not that unity is a marriage that does not have the blessing of God *necessary* for the experience of joy in marriage. Thus we are compelled to consider the command and reason for the restriction of marrying only in the Lord.

A Serious Restriction

Ever since the fall, the institution of marriage has come with a serious restriction for the people of God. When in God's providential care for you it is his purpose that you marry, you are to marry only in the Lord. Our marriages are to be established in such a way that the Lord himself is the Master of our relationship, and that because together we belong to him and are mutually committed to him.

The restriction is not merely that we may only marry those who call themselves Christian, or who go to church—and which church doesn't really matter. That is not a high enough standard for us. Young adults and children need to understand that is not a high enough standard for *them*. To marry "only in the Lord" means that you may only marry one who truly evidences himself or herself as a believer, a member of the bride of Christ, who knows him as Lord of their lives, who desires to walk in the light of his word and to grow in that life.

To put it concretely and somewhat negatively, if you, thinking of marrying, begin a relationship with one who has grown up in the same church but who is not interested in having a serious spiritual conversation, who shows no desire to study God's word and to grow spiritually, that relationship is to end *immediately*. That person does not meet the standard required in marriage.

You must see clear evidence that the person is indeed a child of God and that Christ is *Lord* in his or her life. There may well be a lack of spiritual maturity. There *will* be room for growth. That is something that continues our whole life. But if there is not clear evidence of a desire for spiritual growth, an effort to live in the light of God's word, a love for Christ and his church and his word, then *you don't know* how miserable your life can be should you continue that relationship.

There are many in Christ's church who can tell you of their own sad experience in failing to heed this word of God. I well remember a godly woman, since gone to glory, who in sins of youth had married an unbeliever. God graciously brought her to repentance, and she lived her life in humble submission to her husband, but with all the sorrowful consequences of having to raise a family with no spiritual support from her husband. There could be no spiritual conversations with her husband. Her husband refused to provide for the Christian education of the children and obviously could not help in the spiritual instruction, let alone godly discipline, of the children. Her life was marked by one trial after another, day after day. She would make it a point to speak to the young people about the importance of walking in obedience to God when it comes to establishing relationships that lead to marriage.

The misery of trying to live in a marriage when there is not that unity of faith is immeasurable.

It is striking that in 1 Corinthians 7:39, we find this restriction spoken specifically to women and, even more specifically, to widows. As is clear from all Scripture, this restriction is applicable to *any* man or woman who would marry. But that restriction is evident in the rest of Scripture only from numerous examples of those who violated this divinely established restriction. Here, however, the restriction is explicitly set forth. And it is set forth to women.

This speaks to a temptation that is not exclusive to women, but that nonetheless presses upon women in a unique way. By the nature of their creation and the place God has given them, women are in the position of waiting for a man's leadership in seeking to establish a relationship. It is not easy for us to wait upon God in anything. And because it is the desire of most young women to be married, it is easy to become very impatient when that prospect does not appear.

Furthermore, in Bible times it was common for men to die young. There were many young widows, for whom there was no life insurance and no government provisions. How would they support themselves and their families if they did not remarry? The circumstances of their lives, including the support of their children, often constituted temptations to them even greater than those faced by women who never married.

We must remember that not only is single life not a disease and not a curse, but *not* being married is far better than being in a marriage where there is conflict and a lack of joy. If God does not provide a godly husband with whom you can establish a joyful relationship in the Lord, his will for you is that you patiently wait or that you remain single and focus on the blessedness of your place in the fellowship of Christ's bride. You may marry *only* in the Lord.

But that serious restriction is even more carefully set forth in Amos 3:3, where the rhetorical question is asked, "Can two walk together, except they be agreed?" The expected answer is, "Of course not!" Although that text speaks more broadly than just of marriage, it certainly does apply to marriage. The restriction, therefore, placed upon the one who will marry is that the one whom you will marry must not only be *in the Lord* in a general way, but that you two must be *agreed*.

We must remember what we saw in our consideration of the one-flesh relationship of marriage from Genesis 2:25 as affirmed by Jesus in Matthew 19:5–6. What God joins together in marriage becomes one flesh. That does not just refer to the sexual aspect of marriage. A husband and wife become one flesh in every sense of the word "one." They are of one mind, having the mind of Christ. They are one in purpose, to serve God in every aspect of life. They are one in the faith. Because all these aspects of their unity come to expression, they enjoy each other's fellowship, serve one another, talk to and encourage each other on the pathway of life down which God leads them.

That is so exactly because the holy institution of marriage was created a reflection of the relationship between Christ and the church. For that reason the unity required in marriage is above all a *spiritual* unity. Only that spiritual unity provides the necessary foundation for the expression of unity in the various aspects of married life. Spiritual unity, as that unity comes to expression in *agreement,* is absolutely essential for living joyfully in marriage.

From a practical point of view, we realize that we all fall under the influence of sin and our own sinful flesh. We do not have perfect understanding. Certainly in our youth we have not put everything together when it comes to the application of God's word to daily living. For those brought up in faithful churches and receiving instruction from the word of God throughout childhood and youth, there often is a doctrinal understanding of the basics of biblical truth. But that has to be lived. You must grow in your understanding of the Scriptures and the joy of the gospel in order properly and with wisdom to be able to apply God's word to your daily life.

That is especially true because as children we grow up "under the law" as it were. I do not speak of that as if Christ has not yet fulfilled the law. I refer to the fact that as children we grow up with strict guidelines and boundaries and with much emphasis on the dos and don'ts. The nature of children requires that. But part of growing up is coming to spiritual maturity and understanding the riches of the Christian life in the freedom that is ours in Christ and under the gospel.

In our youth we are usually still developing in our understanding, still breaking free from a legalistic perspective. The Christian life must become more and more a life of thankfulness and the joyful expression of living in love as those who belong to our faithful Savior Jesus Christ. Some, sadly, never progress in their understanding and thus never really experience the joy that is in Christ Jesus. But to live in the joy of the gospel is essential for living joyfully in marriage.

As you establish relationships that might, in God's providence, lead to marriage, there are all kinds of things that you have to talk about—conversations the nature of which will continue in married life. I am not referring merely to things such as your likes and dislikes in food choices. All kinds of spiritual discussions are necessary, discussions about your Christian faith and the application of that faith in your daily life and perspective. That is necessary in order to determine whether you are *agreed* and whether you are prepared to live together and to grow together in the faith and to apply the word of God together in such areas as the particular roles and responsibilities in marriage, in serving each other, in finance and children and child-rearing and so on.

When one member of the relationship, although a Christian as we defined that earlier, comes from a different church background, those differences must be faced *first*, because it is the truth of the word of God that alone sets the foundation for a godly perspective and life. You realize, then, that to marry someone from a different church background adds significantly to the challenges that you face in preparations for marriage.

"Only in the Lord" and "agreed"—a serious restriction to marriage.

The Reason for That Restriction

The reason is very simple. You cannot properly reflect the beauty of marriage to the glory of God, and you cannot experience the joy that God would give us in marriage, without being unified in this way.

Notice how Amos puts the question. He does not ask, "*May* two walk together, except they be agreed?" To that question, the answer also is clearly indicated in Scripture. But Amos—again, under the inspiration of the Holy Spirit—phrases the question this way: "*Can* two walk together, except they be agreed?" (Amos 3:3, emphasis added).

In the context, Amos is addressing the separation from *God* that was seen in Israel. That is especially pertinent to this application to marriage, because we have seen that marriage is itself a reflection of the relationship not only within God himself, but that of God and his people. God often refers to his relationship with his people as a *marriage* relationship, and Israel's departure one of *adultery*. Here he speaks of Israel as the *family* that he had brought out of the land of Egypt, saying, "You only have I known of all the families of the earth" (Amos 3:2). Yet they were not walking in the fellowship of his love.

When men love God, they keep his commandments. His commandments are not grievous to them, but a delight because of their love for him (1 John 5:3). But in this case Israel walked their own way. There was not agreement with the word of God. There was not unity with their husband.

So when Amos asks, "*Can* two walk together, except they be agreed?" the answer is clear. It is *impossible*! The word "can," as you realize, speaks of ability. In a marriage where there is not agreement, and particularly agreement to the word of God and to the application of God's word to our lives, there *cannot* be the unity necessary for living joyfully in marriage.

The emphasis therefore is not only that we must marry *only in the Lord*, but that we must be *agreed*. There must be the same kind of unity that God would have in his people's relationship to him. Understand, the agreement that God requires on the part of his people *to him* is the same agreement found within his own triune being. That unity comes only "in the Lord" (1 Cor. 7:39).

We have considered together the effects of the fall upon marriage and upon relationships also in the church. We have seen that Christ alone by his redemptive work on the cross and by his ongoing work through the Holy Spirit and by the word redeems and restores the relationship of marriage that God established for his people. Christ alone by his redemptive work reconciles the church to God, and thus restores relationships within the church that had been broken by sin.

But that means that to be partakers of the joy of those restored relations—to God and to one another—we must be partakers of Christ and of his life. Otherwise, living joyfully in marriage, whether we talk about our earthly marriages or the marriage between Christ and his church that our marriages represent, is impossible. Christ must be the center of our lives when it comes to our marriages.

Remember, our covenantal fellowship with God is to come to expression. He has purposed it. That is the very reason he created us and reconciled us unto himself. That is the very reason he has given us the ministry of reconciliation—that in being reconciled to him by the wonder of the forgiveness of our sins, we also might bring to expression in our own lives the covenantal fellowship that we now enjoy with our heavenly Father for Jesus' sake. That is what life in the church is about. Marriage is the same. In single life, you have to remember that you are married indeed to Christ, a member of his bride. You must live that way.

Marriage also is to reflect the *true* marriage in which we are united to Christ. That is clearly expressed in the last part of Ephesians 5.

You cannot do that without being one. Just as unity in the church is established only in the truth and in godliness, so it is in marriage. If you take a spouse with whom there is not this spiritual unity in the Lord, with whom there can only be a very superficial agreement and attraction, the sin that you commit will haunt you.

Yes, there are those who by the amazing grace of God are saved after being married. Paul faced that situation quite frequently as he labored to preach the gospel among the Gentiles. In 1 Corinthians 7 he gave specific instruction to those who, after having been saved by the particular and irresistible grace of God, found themselves in that circumstance of being married to an unbeliever. What a trial! In such a situation the calling within marriage is the same as the calling that we face as believers. But when only one is a believer, he or she can only be faithful to his or her own calling. The marriage itself cannot reflect the beauty of the marriage between Christ and the church, and therefore cannot reflect the joy of that relationship. But the believer is called to obedience and to holiness.

That is the case for a threefold purpose. First, that God might be glorified by the obedience of the one to whom he has given the life of his dear Son. Second, that if God be so pleased, he might use the obedience and holiness of the believing spouse for the salvation of the other spouse, as Peter states explicitly in 1 Peter 3:1–2.

The third purpose for which God calls the believing spouse to maintain the marriage bond and to live in obedience and holiness is for the sake of the children. What a nightmare for children to grow up in a home where not only is one spouse unbelieving, but where the supposedly Christian spouse is constantly bickering and striving, instead of living as a Christian. Paul writes in 1 Corinthians 7:14, "For the unbelieving husband is sanctified by the wife, and the unbelieving wife is sanctified by the husband: else were your children unclean; but now are they holy." The clear implication of that text is that the believing spouse is *living* in holiness before God.

No one suffers more than children in homes where the parents live in rebellion against God, striving one with another. When God calls the husband to nourish and cherish his wife, that calling stands even when that newly converted husband's wife is unbelieving and perhaps even contentious because of his new faith. If that calling stands for the man married to an unbeliever, it presses emphatically upon us who claim the life of Christ and who live as one in the Lord. The same holds true for the woman toward her husband.

Young adults need to see how important it is to marry only in the Lord. When God would have the joy of the relationship of Christ and the church reflected in our own homes, would we dare defile that and fill our homes with sorrow? Would we be so consumed with lust and with the idolatry of self that we would take to ourselves a spouse without regard to the requirements of God? If so, we may expect his wrath. As we read in Hebrews 10:31, "It is a fearful thing to fall into the hands of the living God." The same holds true for you, if you have married in the Lord but have forsaken his word to live marriage your own way.

We have no right to live marriage our own way! We have the calling to live as those agreed, as those who humbly bow before the word of God, confessing our sins one to another and seeking together with wholehearted commitment to live in obedience to our heavenly Father.

The Blessedness of Marrying Only in the Lord

The blessedness of marrying only in the Lord is reflected in the marriage of Christ's bride to him and the joy that follows living faithfully in that relationship. Let's not forget, our marriages are to represent the relationship between Christ and the church.

When we live in harmony with God's word by faith in Christ, and therefore in faithfulness to the callings that he gives us, we experience the joy of God's fellowship and favor. As we live and to the degree that we live in the consciousness of belonging to our faithful Savior Jesus Christ and of our Father's love manifested in giving his Son to us in the unbreakable covenantal bond of marriage, we enjoy a comfort in life and death to which no other comfort compares. Isn't that what you desire?

We know what it is to live apart from God. We know the consequences of sin and of refusing to heed the wise instruction of our heavenly Father. We read about them in Deuteronomy 7, where the Lord explicitly forbade his children to marry those from the idolatrous nations around them. "For they will turn away thy son from following me, that they may serve other gods: so will the anger of the LORD be kindled against you, and destroy thee suddenly" (v. 4). Those consequences are not pleasant. They rob us of the joy that only comes in the way of faithful obedience to God's word. The same truth applies to our marriages.

The truth we have seen from this Scripture is foundational to living joyfully in marriage. It is impossible to experience the joy of marriage without submitting to this serious restriction of marrying only in the Lord, of becoming one with a spouse with whom we are *agreed*.

Understand, this is only the foundation. Living joyfully in marriage is not a matter of finding one with whom you are agreed in the faith and living happily ever after. We have our sinful natures to deal with all our life long. We also have the instruction of God's word to follow and to apply to all the various aspects of married life for the entire time God gives us as married couples. Living joyfully in marriage is the fruit of hard work, of faithful obedience to God. But this is foundational, a truth with no exceptions.

That is so because our Lord Jesus Christ takes a bride that is one with him. By God's eternal decree of election in Christ, that bride is one with him.

She is not perfect. He has to make her perfect, cleansing and sanctifying her, so that she more and more reflects the glory of her husband.

But she is a bride with whom Christ shall live in blessed fellowship and unity forevermore. She is a bride who must fulfill God's purpose in revealing his love and covenantal fellowship to those who love him and keep his commandments.

When God's standard is your standard, his blessing is also your blessing. Live in thankfulness to God, bowing before his word, recognizing that his standard is good for you. He who has given you to Christ would also have you live in the blessedness of fellowship with your Redeemer—whether in single life or within marriage.

Chapter 7

TO THE UNMARRIED

7. For I would that all men were even as I myself. But every man hath his proper gift of God, one after this manner, and another after that.

8. I say therefore to the unmarried and widows, it is good for them if they abide even as I.—1 Corinthians 7:7–8

First Corinthians 7:7–8 calls our attention to the place God has given some Christians in single life.

This is a subject that has often been neglected. It is not, I trust you understand, that the single Christian has been neglected in preaching and instruction, for as Christians we are all one and have the same spiritual needs and receive the same spiritual blessings. But just as there is certain instruction that applies in a particular way to married life and to family life, so there is also certain instruction that applies in a particular way to the life of the unmarried Christian. There is also a particular place God has given single Christians in his church, as there are also certain needs that singles have that must not be forgotten in the life of the congregation.

That is why I have also attempted to demonstrate clearly from Scripture that the consideration of marriage also applies to those who are single. The fact is, marriage is only a reflection of *the* marriage between Christ and the church. Therefore, single members of

Christ's church are indeed married to Christ, members of his bride, precious to him *in the particular place he has given them.*

While I do not attempt to excuse the neglect of any significant treatment of single life, it is proper that there be an emphasis on and a regular treatment of marriage and family life. Especially since God instituted marriage at the very beginning of time and uses that holy institution for the bringing forth of children, gathering his church in the generations of believers and their seed, it is natural and right that marriage and the family should receive as much attention as it proportionately receives in holy Scripture.

But to ignore or neglect single life is an oversight without excuse, for the Bible does speak to this particular aspect of life for some of our members. Although not nearly as frequently as it speaks to marriage and family life, it does speak of the unmarried in more passages than we might estimate.

First Corinthians 7 is a key passage in that connection. It is striking that right in the middle of this passage that addresses marriage and answers many questions of various marriage matters, the inspired apostle clearly teaches that single life is honorable for some. Indeed, it is the "proper gift of God" for some. For the sake of those unmarried, including those bereaved of a spouse, the apostle calls attention to the honorable state of single life, for which there is a significant purpose and certain practical implications.

The Honorable State

The apostle makes a powerful statement when he says in 1 Corinthians 7:8, "I say therefore to the unmarried and widows, it is good for them if they abide even as I." That he refers to single life as "good" shows that the Christian who is single occupies an honorable place.

It is important to understand this, lest we fall into the grievous error of looking at the single Christian as occupying a *lesser* place in God's church. The unmarried and the man or woman who has lost his or her spouse must not think of himself or herself as a second-class citizen in God's church.

Some, in doing so and lacking contentment in God's ways, have lost the joy that should characterize the Christian life or have plunged themselves headlong into immeasurable disaster by seeking to escape single life at all cost, even that of entering a relationship God has expressly forbidden.

Single life is honorable and must be understood exactly in that way. The apostle says, "It is good." That word *good* is a Greek word that speaks of that which is beautiful, excellent in character, and therefore honorable. And that which is *good*—let us not forget—is that which is good in *God's* sight!

As we shall see when we consider verse 1 of 1 Corinthians 7, the apostle is responding to something the Corinthians had written him, namely, "It is good for a man not to touch a woman." But the apostle does not endorse a negative view of sexuality as something carnal and dirty. He does not exalt single life *over* marriage. He does not set forth a view of abstaining from sexual relations as itself good or even meritorious. He does nothing of the sort!

The context, which reaches back into the sixth chapter, addresses the sin of fornication, sexual sin, that plagued not only Greek culture but the church at Corinth. The apostle would that all God's people recognize that Christianity is a matter of being *owned by Christ* soul and body. To be a Christian is to confess, "I am not my own. My body is not my own. It is Christ's and therefore is the temple of the Holy Spirit." For that reason fornication is such a serious sin—not in being a *greater* sin than another, but in the *effects*. It is to defile what has been purchased by Christ's blood.

The sexual relationship has been given by God for the marriage relationship alone, because only within that relationship can be expressed the holy intimacy that exists between Christ and his bride.

So important is it to avoid fornication that in most cases a man is to marry, as is a woman. Marriage is good.

But the apostle would have us know that single life is also good. Single life is excellent, beautiful in God's sight. It is not a higher good, as the Roman Catholic Church wrongly teaches. Paul does not devalue marriage as a lesser good or as incompatible with highest spirituality. But as marriage is good, so single life is good.

The only thing that is evil, the opposite of good, is fornication, *any* sexual sin that—by the very nature of the case—defiles that which God has made good, namely, marriage or single life. So good is single life, so excellent and honorable, says Paul, that "I would that all men were even as myself," that is, unmarried (1 Cor. 7:7).

Now, of course, the question arises: how is single life "good"? When we read in Genesis 2:18 that Jehovah God said, "It is not good that the man should be alone," how can the apostle say it is good to be *unmarried*?

That is an especially compelling question to those who are single and who would like *not* to be single. It is very difficult, oftentimes, for a single person to see singleness as good. Instead it can be a great trial, a cause for much distress, even tears.

There are those who have been thrust into singleness by the ungodliness of a marriage partner unlawfully divorcing them. Others have been thrust into singleness by the unfaithfulness of a marriage partner and subsequent divorce. Single life is the only way of life for them; for the Bible, recognizing the permanency of the marriage bond in God's eyes, forbids remarriage when one's divorced spouse is still living. Romans 7:2–3 states that truth clearly, confirming what Jesus said, as recorded in Luke 16:18 and several other passages: "Whosoever putteth away his wife, and marrieth another, committeth adultery: and whosoever marrieth her that is put away from her husband committeth adultery." The Christian who happens to bear the trial of a failed or corrupted marriage is compelled to find peace with God in single life.

There are others whom God has thrust into single life through the death of a spouse. A person in that state has the right to remarry. As Paul writes in verse 39 of this same chapter, 1 Corinthians 7, "The wife is bound by the law as long as her husband liveth; but if her husband be dead, she is at liberty to be married to whom she will; only in the Lord." To the widow or widower is the freedom to marry again "in the Lord." But the apostle also states that in such a case, single life is *good*. How can that be?

Then there are those men who feel that singleness has been thrust upon them. It is not by choice. Perhaps they have even faced rejection—for whatever reason.

And what about the many single women who long for marriage? The man who is to be a husband must also be, at least in some measure, a leader, the head of the home. He should demonstrate that trait from the beginning. But where the man is expected to take the initiative, has the single young woman any choice? Besides putting herself in a favorable situation of meeting godly young men, what can she do short of flinging herself at a man? So she waits, sometimes very impatiently, sometimes with much sorrow. And single life is *good*?! How so?

The excellence, the goodness, of the state of single life is found in both the text and context of this chapter.

Single life is good and honorable, first, because it is a gift of God to his people. In the words of the text, "Every man hath his proper gift of God, one after this manner, and another after that" (1 Cor. 7:7). God gives the gift of single life to some and the gift of marriage to others. But while marriage is a natural desire, the gift of marriage is not given to all who would like to be married, nor is the gift of singleness given to all those who may be content to be single. No matter our desires, the state in which God places us is a *gift*. That is the emphasis of the text. When the apostle speaks of a "gift," the word used speaks explicitly of a gift of grace, a gift given in divine favor and love to those who are his. You understand now, I am not speaking about how we *receive* it; I am speaking about what it *is*. Singleness, says the Scripture, is a gracious gift of God to some of his own.

Whether we can see or understand it as such, we must acknowledge that single life is a gracious gift of God, for so the Bible teaches us. It is therefore *not* a curse, *not* a disease, *not* something to cause one to feel less loved by God. Singleness, as a gracious gift of God, is an honorable state. For that reason, single life should not be looked upon as merely "giving up," but rather as a "taking on," the *receiving* of a gift from our gracious and merciful heavenly Father.

Second, single life is honorable inasmuch as marriage belongs only to this passing age, and thus is not an absolute requirement for God's people. The apostle, understanding this, found single life not only rewarding, but in his case preferable to marriage. That marriage belongs only to this passing age finds emphasis in 1 Corinthians 7:29–31:

29. But this I say, brethren, the time is short: it remaineth, that both they that have wives be as though they had none;
30. And they that weep, as though they wept not; and they that rejoice, as though they rejoiced not; and they that buy, as though they possessed not;
31. And they that use this world, as not abusing it: for the fashion of this world passeth away.

Mind you, the apostle sets forth that reality right in the midst of this whole consideration of marriage. Marriage belongs to this present life, which is very quickly passing away. That affirms what Christ taught in Luke 20:34–35, as recorded also by Matthew and Mark: "The children of this world marry, and are given in marriage:

but they which shall be accounted worthy to obtain that world, and the resurrection from the dead, neither marry, nor are given in marriage." Marriage serves some in their earthly sojourn. Marriage is a good gift to some. And as is evident from the fact that God instituted marriage even before the fall into sin, marriage itself is a good institution, not something merely carnal. But it is not an everlasting institution, as is the relationship between Christ and the church, and as is *our* relationship with *Christ*.

In that light we must understand that marriage is not a requirement for the Christian. Yes, marriage is required for sexual relations. But marriage itself is not a requirement. That is the apostle's point in 1 Corinthians 7:6, when he says, "But I speak this by permission, and not of commandment." Do not misunderstand that statement. That remark does not undermine the authority of his inspired instruction. He is reflecting back upon the instruction of the first five verses. He has just exhorted men and women in the church to avoid fornication by marrying and so bringing to expression their sexuality *only* within that holy institution. Some might suppose that such is a command to all men and women in the church without exception. But the apostle makes clear that such would be a wrong conclusion to what he has written.

To marry is not commanded but *permitted*. There is another option, an honorable option for the Christian man or woman. That is to serve the Lord in single life, rather than in marriage. So Paul says, "For I would that all men were even as I myself" (1 Cor. 7:7). And in verse 8, "I say therefore to the unmarried and widows, it is good for them if they abide even as I." Again, it is *good*, it is beautiful in God's sight. It is indeed his gracious gift to some, though not to all.

The Significant Purpose

Implied in the truth of single life as a good gift of God to some is the fact that single life has a significant purpose. Whether marriage or single life, each is a gift. It is for God to determine which good gift he will give to each one—for his own purpose. Marriage is not an end in itself; nor is single life an end in itself. In whatever God's gift for your life and mine, whether married or single life, that gift is one of the means God uses to sanctify us and to lead us to heaven.

The apostle, before going on later in this chapter to spell out the significant purpose of single life, would simply point to himself and his own experience. Having received this proper gift of God, he was living his life as one unmarried. He knew what it was to be single. He was not writing merely theoretically. For one thing, Paul wrote as inspired by the Holy Spirit. The word he wrote therefore was perfect and authoritative both for the church at Corinth and for the church today for which that word has been preserved. But we note that the inspired apostle also wrote from his own experience.

We would read too much into the spiritual life of the apostle if we would assume that he never struggled with single life. It would be far more likely that also his singleness came under this testimony, as Paul wrote in Philippians 4:11: "I have learned, in whatsoever state I am, therewith to be content." But he saw the purpose of his own singleness and recognized that single life was the good purpose of God for him.

Let us be very clear that the purpose of single life is *not* to live a carefree life of personal freedom and self-seeking. That is never the God-given purpose for any Christian's life. The person who lives in that way shows a spiritual emptiness or void that is tragic. This must be stated because we live in such perilous times, when men are lovers of their own selves, as we read in 2 Timothy 3. In the self-centeredness of our culture, it is easy for us and for our young adults to get caught up in the phenomena of covetousness and pleasure madness that forsakes divinely instituted callings and stations of life. Sociologists recognize the growing number of those who live single lives. There are any number of reasons for those rising numbers. But among those reasons in the *world* are those things of which we have been warned in Scripture, including a growing rejection of biblical standards concerning marriage and family life, let alone single life, and the increasing prevalence and acceptance of fornication, by which—in defiance of marriage—men and women look for pleasure without obligation. Self-seeking becomes the norm where God's standards are cast aside.

But those evils also enter the church. For that reason we must understand that the purpose of single life is not that we can avoid the responsibilities of marriage and family in order to have more time to seek our own pleasures in life. The purpose of single life is not to be able to escape the financial burdens of family life, to be able to grow wealthy unhindered by the responsibilities of providing for a wife and children. The purpose of single life is not to be able to continue to seek the pleasures of life and buy what I want when I want it. In the world, that is commonly done—especially because it has become so easy to fulfill one's sexual desires outside the bond of marriage. I say again, if that is the thinking of any person in the church, that one had better examine carefully his or her relationship with God. The person who lives that way shows a spiritual emptiness.

Positively, the purpose of single life—as is true with the entire Christian life in whatever state—is to live to God's glory, to bring to expression and to live in the joy of our marriage to Christ.

In this case, the purpose is to live to God's glory in singleness. That is what Paul goes on to emphasize in this chapter, pointing out that the unmarried Christian is able to devote his or her life to God in a way not possible by the one who is married. Singleness is to be seen by us as useful to the kingdom of heaven.

The apostle expresses the great desire that the Christian have a life free of concerns: "But I would have you *without carefulness*," that is, free from anxiety (1 Cor. 7:32, emphasis added). That freedom from anxiety is more positively stated as, I would have you able to focus on your spiritual life and your relationship to the Lord, or as we read in verse 35, "that ye may attend upon the Lord without distraction."

The passage tells us that single life is most conducive to that spiritual focus. That does not mean that there are not distractions in single life. Of course there are. Especially is that the case when we do not see the good in singleness or are not content in God's ways with us. Especially are the distractions great when we live in the perspective of "the grass is greener on the other side of the fence," a contemporary way of expressing discontent and covetousness. And the very fact that we live in a world where we are surrounded by distractions makes single life no different from married life from that limited point of view.

But by the very nature of the case, married life is far more demanding and distracting to spiritual life. That is because—and let us understand this well—marriage is the most intimate and demanding of all human relationships and commitments. The apostle, while writing extensively in this chapter and elsewhere about the high calling of marriage, has a keen awareness of the responsibilities, burdens, and trials of married life. Those who are married understand this, or should. Those who intend to be married *must* realize this.

Marriage is the most intimate and demanding of all human relationships and commitments. The married person focuses a tremendous amount of attention upon spouse and children—and must. That is the peculiar calling of married life. But that brings a huge need, not only, but greater *difficulty* in maintaining a primary commitment to Christ, which lies at the very heart of our spiritual life and activity.

The unmarried person, on the other hand, is given by God the peculiar opportunity, according to verse 32, to care for the things of the Lord, how he may please the Lord. That is the purpose of single life when given as God's gift to a particular number of his people.

The apostle, no doubt, had in mind several particular vocations that the single person could occupy in great usefulness to the church. There was a great need, after all, for those who would give themselves to the Lord's work—whether as laborers in Christ's vineyard, unmarried ministers and missionaries, in the care of the sick, or assisting in the homes of those mothers with large families or helping in the education of the children—to mention but a few examples.

In our day the vocational opportunities are many times broader than in the apostle's day. Nor is the single Christian limited to a particular field of work. Any child of God, married or single, man or woman, has the calling to look upon his particular vocation and calling as the place in which he is called to serve the Lord. But the single person *ought to have* more time to serve and to participate in the life and needs of the church. You who are in that honorable state ought not hesitate to look for such opportunities and to seize them. It is not good when our singles neglect attendance at Bible studies and other church activities. It is not good for you, nor for the congregation. You are an important part of Christ's bride, an important member of the church, called to participate in and contribute to the life of the congregation in as many ways as possible. God has given you a peculiar place and calling as members of Christ's body.

The Practical Implications

That brings us to some practical implications of this divine instruction concerning the life of the single Christian.

First, we need to understand the important place that unmarried Christians occupy in Christ's church. If we receive the Bible's teaching on single life, then we will understand that in single life a child of God occupies a high calling. It might be, consequently, that our way of thinking needs to undergo some change.

When we understand this biblical teaching, we will no longer look upon single life as something to pity or to look down upon. The unmarried members of the church, while being included in our prayers, are not to be prayed for in the category of those who are sick and dying. They bear trials, like any Christian. But their way as singles is not a shameful way nor a way that should cast doubt upon their character. Singleness is not a mark of failure or inferiority. It is rather the gift of God for some. Recognizing that, we ought to embrace singles for what they contribute to the life of the church. That means not only welcoming them into our homes when we visit and including them in our activities, but encouraging them in that particular place they can occupy in the life of church and school. And where some singles neglect their calling, we must remind them of the high place they occupy as members of the body of Christ.

Second, you who are single must understand your place and calling. For some that single life will not be permanent. For others the gift of God to you and your calling is to carry on in that honorable state. That means not only must there be an understanding of these things, but there must be *acceptance*. To accept is to understand with a view to a changed life. It is to grasp these glorious truths with a view to acting upon them.

There is an understanding here that single life often bears its own peculiar difficulty, and particularly a difficulty in acceptance. To live the single life, one must have the gift of self-control over sexual desire. Those lacking such self-control are to marry. But even with that qualification, there are many who say, "But I don't feel I have that special gift, and yet I have no prospect of marriage. What then am I to do?"

Acceptance is not only to accept intellectually that God calls some to single life, but to act upon that reality. That begins not simply by refraining from fornication and resigning yourself to your singleness with discontent, but by living your life believing that singleness is God's *gift*—at least at this particular time in your life.

Third, God would teach us that true contentment and joy are to be found exactly where he places us at any given period in our life. Paul puts it this way in verse 24 of this chapter: "Brethren, let every man, wherein he is called, therein abide *with* God." Notice that. The Lord who loves us in Christ Jesus has drawn certain lines around our lives. He orders where we shall live and the family in which we shall grow up. He determines whether we are rich or poor or somewhere in between. He gives health or sickness and the characteristics of our nature and personality. He is also the one who sovereignly determines if and when we shall be single or married. It is only within those divinely appointed boundaries and in humble submission to God's perfect wisdom that we can find true contentment.

The key to our happiness is bowing before God's sovereignty and confessing with Psalm 18:30, "His way is perfect." Then remember also this: When you are single and want to be married, God is not asking you to *dispose* of that desire. He does not call you to say, "I'm guilty of carrying this improper desire." Rather, he would have you take that natural desire and cling to him *with* that desire, so that he gives you to see your particular place and gives you to experience contentment even while carrying that natural desire.

Finally, the single life is to be enjoyed and used. Single life, while constituting a trial for some, is not to be viewed simply as a cross to bear but as an opportunity to serve.

We can also call attention to this same truth from a more negative perspective. When we are discontent with God's ways for us, when we always see the negative of single life—to apply it now to this particular text we are considering—then genuine love for God and others no longer guides our choices. Discontent clouds our vision and makes it impossible to glorify God and live in the joy of his fellowship. If we spend all our energy pursuing that which our hearts covet, we are consuming negatively the energy that we should properly be using in serving God with lives of gratitude.

It has often been said that one of the best preparations for marriage is to learn contentment in single life. There is truth to that statement. The truth is found in the fact that contentment recognizes the work of God in weaving together my life. Contentment sees the love of God in Christ and knows that in his own perfect way God is making something very beautiful of my life—and that in connection with his whole church. Knowing that the end result of all his work in Christ Jesus is beautiful, perfect, I can rejoice and be thankful even before seeing the finished work.

Paul experienced the advantages of singleness—for personal holiness, for detachment from the world, for wholehearted commitment to the Lord. How often have not single members of Christ's church been also main contributors to the financial causes of the churches and schools? In what way can *you* serve as an unmarried member of Christ's body? Let us remember that in whatever place and calling we find ourselves by God's sovereign appointment, we have one fundamental calling—that is to glorify God and to enjoy him forever. May each of us know that place and fulfill that calling—for Christ's sake.

Part 2

Privileged to Make It Work

Chapter 8

THE PERMANENCE OF THIS MOMENTARY MARRIAGE

2. For the woman which hath an husband is bound by the law to her husband so long as he liveth; but if the husband be dead, she is loosed from the law of her husband.

3. So then if, while her husband liveth, she be married to another man, she shall be called an adulteress: but if her husband be dead, she is free from that law; so that she is no adulteress, though she be married to another man.

—Romans 7:2–3

This chapter begins a new section of *Living Joyfully in Marriage*. Having seen from Scripture the foundational truths concerning marriage, or what I referred to as the essentials of joyful marriage, I now call attention to a few texts that establish for us reasons to make it work. When we think of reasons for doing something, we often consider the benefits or advantages to ourselves. I don't intend to be so self-focused in this section. We need to look more deeply at some of the foundational principles for which God has established marriage. The reasons to live joyfully in marriage all flow out of God's divine purpose in the institution of holy marriage as a reflection of the glorious covenantal relationship between Christ and the church. Only in that consciousness will we labor to make our marriages reflect the mystery of Christ and the church.

The first reason to devote ourselves to making our marriages reflect the joy of *the* marriage between Christ and the church is what the Bible teaches us concerning the permanence of our momentary earthly marriages. The marriage between Christ and his bride is ever-lasting. It embraces all who are in Christ Jesus by the election of grace and through faith, married or unmarried and no matter your particular circumstance in this earthly life. But the marriages that God has established for some of us in this earthly sojourn, marriages also used oftentimes for the gathering of his church from the children of these marriages, are only *temporary* relationships. They last only until death parts us. That is emphasized in Romans 7:2–3. It is emphasized for the purpose of establishing another divine truth pertinent to every one of us, namely, the freedom that is ours in Christ Jesus.

A Binding Relationship

By referring to the *permanence* of this momentary marriage, I am calling attention to the humanly unbreakable nature of the marriage relationship. As Romans 7:2 puts it, "The woman which hath an husband is *bound* by the law to her husband *so long as he liveth*" (emphasis added).

Earthly marriage as God himself established and defined it, as the relationship between one man and one woman, is a *binding* relationship. It is such a binding relationship that only death can break it. Marriage vows commit us to reflecting the relationship of Christ and his church! Such a binding and intimate relationship is also a reason to be faithful to our callings and to each other as husbands and wives. The fact that there is no exit to the marriage relationship is a powerful incentive to maintaining a healthy relationship. Living joyfully in marriage is something we desire not just for the honeymoon or for the first year of marriage, but for all the years that we have together as husbands and wives.

The apostle points out that the marriage relationship illustrates a universal truth. The law has dominion over a man as long as he lives. That the law has dominion speaks of that which *binds* us, as is evident from the language the apostle uses in Romans 7:2. Dominion speaks of bondage. It speaks of being held in such a way that there is no freedom. In verse 6 Paul speaks of the contrast that comes by virtue of our deliverance in Christ. By the wonder of God's grace in Christ Jesus we have been delivered from the law wherein we *were* held. The emphasis is on the binding relationship of the law, and therefore of marriage as it serves as an illustration of that binding relationship.

While it is not my purpose in this chapter to develop the main thesis of the apostle in Romans 7, it is necessary to understand what the apostle is addressing, so that we better understand the particular illustration that we are considering.

Paul had demonstrated earlier, in Romans 3:20, that by the works of the law no man shall be justified in the sight of God. In this chapter, following the instruction of chapter 6, he is expanding upon the truth that, as it is impossible to be justified by the law, so it is impossible to be sanctified by the law. In fact, he would have us understand that the law, separated from the gospel, is a hindrance to sanctification. To remove the focus from Christ and to set before the church the dos and don'ts of the law is to magnify their condemnation and to rob them of their joy.

What is necessary, the inspired apostle says, is to recognize the change in our relationship to the law and to God himself. Where we once were married to the law, bound to it even unto death, that relationship to the law is now broken by what Christ has done on the cross. You are become dead to the law by the body of Christ. And why? In order that you should be lawfully married to another, even to him who is raised from the dead. But why should we be married to this other? If death has freed us from that binding relationship in which we were miserable, why should we be married to another, and in particular to Christ? The last part of Romans 7:4 gives the answer: "that we should bring forth fruit unto God."

God purposes that our marriage to Christ be *fruitful* to the glory of his own name. The relationship in which we stand to Christ, then, causes us to look at the law in a different light. As those married to Christ, we now stand before the perfect law of liberty, as the law that guides us in the life we desire to live, a life of gratitude to the one to whom we are married. Indeed, there is only one way to be fruitful unto God, and that is to be married to Christ and to live in the knowledge of the beauty of that relationship. It is to live with such a focus upon our Bridegroom that we shout in exaltation, "I thank God through Jesus Christ our Lord" (Rom. 7:25)! Then our lives become an expression of our love for him. That is the main thrust of the apostle's instruction here.

But our focus now is upon the illustration he uses under the inspiration of the Holy Spirit to demonstrate this truth. "The woman which hath an husband is bound by the law to her husband so long as he liveth" (Rom. 7:2).

Our marriages involve us in binding relationships. The relationship of marriage is as inescapable as is our relationship to the law. That means the relationship of husband and wife is binding before God until death parts us. Only death makes that separation.

Many in our day take the position that divorce makes the separation. To divorce is to put that marriage relationship to death. That is the argument you hear in churches where remarriage has been permitted and even encouraged in cases where there has been divorce. The unbelieving world does not argue that way. To those outside the church there is no equating of divorce with death. To the world it is just a matter of "things not working out," and therefore "moving on." But the church stands squarely before the many passages of the Bible that forbid divorce except, as we read in Matthew 19:9, in the case of fornication, and even there not using the term "divorce" but rather "putting away." In addition, many passages clearly forbid remarriage of the one who either has put away his or her spouse or who has been put away by his or her spouse. Those passages cannot simply be discarded. So those who would attempt to make room for remarriage after divorce would say, "To divorce is to put that marriage to death."

There is a problem with such an interpretation, however. Divorce is the act of man. Divorce therefore cannot be synonymous with death. Death is executed by God. God is the one who alone takes life from us at his appointed time and for his appointed purpose. Furthermore, when it comes to marriage, Jesus said, "What therefore God hath joined together, let not man put asunder" (Mark 10:9). Only God himself has the right to put asunder. Only God can put asunder. He does that in death.

The bond of marriage is humanly inescapable.

That is evident, for one thing, by the language the apostle uses here: "The woman which hath an husband is bound by the law to her husband" (Rom. 7:2). The term *bound* is a perfect tense verb that speaks of ongoing action. We might correctly translate it this way: "The woman which hath an husband is *permanently bound* by the law to her husband." That bond goes on and on and on, until death breaks the bond.

That is evident too from what this figure serves to illustrate. The law has dominion over a man as long as he lives. Those who say that the bond of marriage can be broken by the will of man destroy the truth that Paul illustrates. Think of this. There are those who say, "I am not bound by any law. No one is going to tell me what to do. I will live as I well please." Does that attitude make him free from the law? It certainly does not.

LIVING JOYFULLY IN MARRIAGE

The truth that the apostle sets forth is universally true throughout human society. The relationship of men and women everywhere
to the law of the land is one of being bound. The laws of our country
bind us, every one of us. To violate the law brings consequences. The
consequences will generally be proportionate to the severity of the
violation of the law. But the consequences demonstrate our bondage
to the law. The man who says, "The law cannot touch me," might
live in brazen rebellion against that law. But he is not free. In fact,
the moment he violates that law, the authorities will be after him to
reveal clearly that he is not free. There is only one way we shall be
free from the law. The moment we die the law can say nothing to us.
The law cannot hold a dead man accountable.

Now Paul says, in confirmation of all God's word, "The same is
true of marriage."

2. For the woman which hath an husband is bound by the
   law to her husband so long as he liveth; but if the husband
   be dead, she is loosed from the law of her husband.
3. So then if, while her husband liveth, she be married to
   another man, she shall be called an adulteress: but if her
   husband be dead, she is free from that law; so that she
   is no adulteress, though she be married to another man.
   (Rom. 7:2–3)

That means you have reason to make your marriage what it
ought to be, because you are going to be together until death parts
you. To find another spouse is not an option—lest you become an
adulterer or adulteress for whom the kingdom of heaven is closed
except there be repentance. And repentance includes a turning from
the sin. There is no escaping what we read in this passage and the
consequence as expressed in 1 Corinthians 6:9–10.

There have been many times when, sadly, marriages did not
honor God and did not reflect the relationship of Christ and the

church but defiled it. When couples, seeing the hard work necessary to make their marriage what it must be, might have been inclined to give up and to divorce and marry another, this truth of God's word in Romans 7:2–3 provided an incentive to invest the necessary labor toward bringing that marriage into a faithful reflection of Christ and the church. If you are married, your marriage, given you by God, binds you together in God's sight until death parts you. You must see to it that you walk together faithfully and in obedience to God's word, that your marriage reflects the mystery of Christ and the church and does not desecrate that glorious relationship.

That is the law of marriage that binds us. That is the earthly permanence of these binding relationships—as inescapable as the law that has dominion over us as long as we live.

A Momentary Relationship

We are to commit ourselves to that calling of faithful obedience, realizing that our marriages are *momentary* relationships. Death dissolves the relationship.

This illustration, by its very nature, serves to show the tremendous inferiority of our marriages to that marriage of Christ to his bride. Earthly marriage in its most beautiful expression pales in comparison to the relationship in which you stand to Christ by faith.

Once again, from that point of view, those who are single and who stand in a living relationship to Christ by faith have a far better relationship than that of marriage. Our union with Christ is not subject to death, ever. Our relationship to Christ is a treasure, the riches of which only become more valuable to us, even into eternity. While we strive to make our marriages a faithful reflection of that beautiful relationship, and must do so, the fact remains that death hovers over our marriages.

The apostle, by this illustration, points to the fact that marriage, while binding and bearing permanence so long as that husband and wife have breath, is nonetheless a momentary relationship. Our relationships in marriage are temporary. So strongly does the apostle emphasize that truth that we find in the last part of Romans 7:5 that when our marriages are likened to the law, we only bring forth fruit unto death. That is humbling, is it not?

Given the fact, as we read in the last part of verse 4, that the object of our marriage to Christ is that we might bring forth fruit unto *God*, we must understand that our marriages, instituted to reflect that wonderful relationship of Christ and his bride, are also then to bring forth fruit unto God. That is the ultimate purpose of our marriages, that we might bring forth fruit unto God. It is not to gratify myself and my lusts. Marriage is not what I might get out of it. The purpose of marriage is not to have another serve me or be enslaved to me. The purpose is that we might serve each other and serve together to the glory of God. That is true in our bearing of children, when that is God's way for us. That is true in the rearing of children. But that is true in every aspect of married life, also as that married life is lived and nurtured in the bosom of the church and by the preaching of the gospel. God would have us bring forth fruit unto him. In that way, living out of Christ and serving God, we live joyfully in marriage.

But the text also emphasizes that the only way we can do that is by being married to Christ. So long as we are married to the law, it is impossible to bring forth fruit unto God. The illustration of marriage used by the inspired apostle here reminds us of the effects of sin in our very natures. Everything we do in married life bears fruit—for good or evil. But the end of it all is death. That is the humbling and inescapable reality of our marriages. They are momentary relationships.

Death ends the marriage relationship and releases the surviving spouse for a new relationship. Notice, whether one enters a new relationship is not the question here. The apostle addresses that matter in 1 Corinthians 7. To remarry is not required and in many cases is not even preferable. But death frees the surviving spouse from that relationship in which he or she was bound.

That is how the text illustrates the wonder of our having been freed from the bondage of the law, that we might be married to *Christ* and live in the consciousness of the beauty of our relationship to him. To live out of mere compulsion, to live even in marriage as a slave to the demands of a spouse, rather than out of love, is to live in a relationship with no joy and much bitterness. To live in the fullness of our relationship to Christ is the end, the purpose, of all that God has determined for your life and mine.

Marriage is not the ultimate goal of our lives. Marriage only *serves* some men and women to that end. That marriage is not the end is evident from the fact that death ends the marriage relationship. In death, God himself tells us that the purpose in our marriages is accomplished. Our earthly marriages fall away as a reminder that they are only reflections of the marriage that alone can last and of which we who are in Christ Jesus are *all* partakers.

To whomsoever God gives marriage, he gives it with the purpose, even the law, that we assist one another on the pathway to heaven. Our relationships are to be marked by love, love that is expressed in giving one to another and seeking one another's welfare, even as Christ and the church. That is why our marriages can only be enjoyed to the degree that we are living with our focus on *the* marriage between Christ and the church.

The contrast that the apostle emphasizes here is profound, that of being dead or alive. Do not overlook that. This truth underlies not just how we live in marriage, but how we live *period*. What marks us as Christians is not something superficial. To be a Christian does not mean that you clean up your life a little, that you make a few repairs in marriage and whatever other relationships you realize are marred. Some conceive of Christianity in those terms. We must be told to do certain things and to avoid other things, so that we can make some improvements and live a better life than what we were living. It is certainly true, as demonstrated by the New Testament church, that the Christian life will bring changes in how we live. Those changes were a profound testimony of God's grace in the early church. But those changes are not what makes a Christian.

The Christian is defined by being made alive in Christ Jesus, by being married to Christ and becoming therefore a *new creature* (2 Cor. 5:17). That is not something superficial. That is possessing the life of the risen Christ. It is having a heart that is one with God, that seeks his face, that longs to hear his word, that delights to do his will, and that immediately knows when I have failed him and offended him. It is a bond that our marriages can only reflect. And if our marriages and our lives are not reflecting that, it is not because we have not been told how the life of Christ comes to expression in those who are his. Rather, it is because we are not living in the glorious light of the face of the risen Lord. Our *hearts* are not right. We have closed our ears to his word and to his call to repentance.

It does not matter how good our lives appear. If our hearts are right with God, we are not going to be seeking our own thing, proud of our morality, of our good works, and looking down upon other people, including our spouses. If our hearts are right with God, we have a single-minded focus, namely, to bring forth fruit unto God. That is to serve in humble gratitude of heart, seeking the welfare of our spouse or our fellow believers, as we walk the pathway toward heaven. Scripture does not describe this as something that is possible, if only we work hard enough at it. This bearing fruit unto God is the inevitable result of being married to Christ. What we *could not do*, so long as we were married to the law, we *do* by virtue of being one with the risen Savior.

Marriage to Christ is such a union that *his* life flows through us. As his life flows through us by his Holy Spirit, it also stimulates our growth and our desire to please God in all things. That is the relationship our marriages are to reflect, and yet can *only* reflect.

A Purposeful Relationship

Though earthly marriage is momentary, the permanence of this momentary relationship serves a beautiful purpose. It serves to emphasize that our marriage to Christ, and his to us, is an eternal union. The God and Father of our Lord Jesus Christ has chosen us in him before the foundation of the world (Eph. 1:4). In Christ we have redemption through his blood, even the forgiveness of sins (Col. 1:14). And Christ has done so that he might sanctify and cleanse us his bride and present her to himself a glorious church (Eph. 5:26–27). Our marriage to Christ is from eternity to eternity! In an earthly way, the beauty of our marriage to Christ is reflected in the permanence of our earthly marriages. And the joy of that union with Christ is to be reflected in our marriages.

Those of us who marry enter that relationship knowing that we face a trial that one who is unmarried will not face. There is to come a tearing apart of our marriages in death. That is inevitable. While in our youth we do not think about that very often, especially as we get older we realize more and more the momentary nature of our marriages.

But our glorious marriage to Christ is far superior! That union is *eternal!* There is no fear of death destroying that relationship. There is no fear to hinder the development of this beautiful relationship to our exalted Savior. That relationship, the marriage to which we *all* belong, will not end! It is eternal.

Why is that? Because we are married to him who alone conquered death. He has risen! The resurrection gospel, when understood and embraced by faith, stands as the reason to make our marriages work, to live joyfully in marriage. We want our marriages to reflect what God intended them to reflect—the permanence of our relationship to the risen Lord. The church has become the bride of him who is raised from the dead! Do you understand the importance of that?

Christ's death was necessary. It was the dowry, as it were, paid to make us his bride. Nothing less was acceptable to God than the payment of Christ's precious blood. That is what it took to cleanse us and to clothe us with the white robes of righteousness, the glorious garments of Christ's bride. But that Christ died for us could not be the last word. If death were the last word, we might be freed from the law, but we would be widowed! There would be no joy, no gain. The church is the bride of him who has risen from the dead!

The apostle's point, therefore, is that Christ has given to us the life that the law could never give. When we hear the voice of the law saying, "Do this, and you shall live," we look to Christ and respond to the law, "I have a life that you can never give. I am married to the risen Christ. I live in the joy of my union with him. I have a heavenly Father who in eternity conceived of a marriage for me. He conceived of Christ as the bridegroom and the entire church as his bride, with me a living member thereof."

Because the church has become dead to the law and has been married to the risen Christ, she brings forth fruits of the joy of that life. How beautiful is that marriage! How blessed is my place in the joy of that relationship! In that light, I live in my relationship to my wife, guided by the word of God. The joy that is mine in Christ Jesus is reflected in our relationship.

The godly wife does not say to her husband, any more than the church would say to Christ, "I've done this and this and this for you; what are you going to do for me?" No. She gives willingly. She lives for her husband, because she lives for Christ. And the godly husband, even as Christ, shows his love and cares for his wife, recognizing her as the weaker vessel, giving honor to her whom God gave to him.

That is the Christian life, living in the joy of our Lord, serving him in love in whatever place and calling he gives us.

That is also Christian marriage, marriage that reflects the joy of being united with Christ, partakers of the freedom he purchased for us. That is God's purpose for you who are married. That is a reason to dedicate yourself to making your marriage what it ought to be. But that also will be the fruit of the Spirit's work in you who belong to your faithful Savior Jesus Christ. For to be married to Christ is to bring forth fruit unto God.

Chapter 9

PRIVILEGED TO REFLECT THE MYSTERY

This is a great mystery: but I speak concerning Christ and the church.—Ephesians 5:32

Ephesians 5:32 may well be the most important and most profound of all the texts in Scripture that reflect upon the marriage relationship. For one thing, it gives us the all-important reminder that Jesus Christ is to be the focal point of our lives. That is a dominant theme in Paul's epistles. There is no Christian life apart from a personal relationship, a faith union, with Jesus Christ. There is no life for the church apart from that covenantal union with the eternal Son of God who became flesh to take the church as his bride. So the Holy Spirit, true to Jesus' words in John 15:26, always testifies of *Christ*, doing so also through the inspired apostle Paul, and showing who Christ is to us and how his life and love come to expression in and through his bride and the members of that bride.

Ephesians 5:32 reminds us that the most important relationship in life, the most blessed revelation of the covenant into which God has taken us, is found not in marriage, but in that which marriage is to reflect. This is why a book on marriage is applicable to all the members of the church and not just those who are married.

Marriage is to reflect the relationship that we enjoy in and with Christ Jesus, the great bridegroom of the church. It is that glorious relationship that is our only comfort in life and death. It is that glorious relationship that affects our entire perspective in life. It is in the consciousness of that relationship—and only in that consciousness—that we shall live in the thankfulness of seeking God's will in every aspect of our lives. But that glorious relationship between Christ and the church is a relationship that those who are married are privileged to reflect in the joyful union of holy marriage. That privilege, understood by us when we have a biblical, Christ-centered focus in our lives, is also motivation that our marriages are faithful in modeling Christ and the church.   *ie exclusive.*

That we are privileged to reflect the mystery of Christ and the church is reason to see to it that we are living joyfully in marriage.

A Great Privilege

What a great privilege is set before us in Ephesians 5:32 when we see it in the context of the entire section of verses 22–33. Marriage has been designed by God to mirror the covenant between Christ and the church.

The context here has the apostle setting forth the marriage relationship under the inspiration of the Holy Spirit. Not to be overlooked is how the apostle has come to consider marriage. In Ephesians, as with all his epistles, he begins by setting forth the heart of the gospel. In the first three chapters he unfolds the wonder of the life that is ours entirely by the grace of God revealed in Christ Jesus, and that according to God's eternal purpose to take us into his own household by adopting us through Jesus Christ to himself. It is important for us to see that, especially in connection with Paul's reference in our text to the *mystery*.

That term *mystery* has confused some, especially because the Roman Catholic Church has interpreted it *sacrament*. But the term, which is correctly, even phonetically, translated as *mystery*, refers to a divine secret that God has revealed by his Spirit. The term is used elsewhere to refer to other revelations of the wonder of salvation or the kingdom of God. Think, for example, of the mysteries of the kingdom Jesus revealed in the parables.

The term *mystery*, therefore, refers to that which God makes known of his *covenant*. It is a truth for which we were not looking, a truth so wonderful it can only be revealed by the Holy Spirit. I am reminded of Psalm 25:14, where with Hebrew parallelism the covenant is defined in terms of God revealing his secret to those who fear him. "The secret of the LORD is with them that fear him; and he will show them his covenant."

To know the fellowship and love of God himself, to enjoy that profound and wonderful truth of God's covenant, is only ours by the Spirit of Christ applying the gospel to our hearts. John writes in his first epistle, in 1 John 1:3, "That which we have seen and heard declare we unto you, that ye also may have fellowship with us: and truly our fellowship is with the Father, and with his Son Jesus Christ." Then follows this: "And these things write we unto you, that your joy may be full" (v. 4). The mystery of God's covenant is the source of our joy. Apart from living in the consciousness of our fellowship with God in Jesus Christ, joy will escape us. It cannot be ours.

The same is true in marriage. If our marriages are to be expressions of joy, our lives must be grounded in our relationship to Jesus Christ. We must be living in consciousness of being married to *Christ*, partakers of his covenantal life. That is the chief relationship.

Our text speaks of that union between Christ and the church as the *mega*-mystery, the great mystery. The marriage to Christ is the most extraordinary, most blessed relationship that a person can have. That is why to be single is not to have a lesser place, when you realize your union with Christ. When you have that relationship, you have a relationship far greater than marriage, the relationship that marriage can only faintly reflect.

The blessedness of being one with Christ is emphasized throughout this epistle. Already in the first chapter of Ephesians, Paul spoke of these things in terms of God "having made known unto us the mystery of his will" (v. 9). In chapter 3, he revealed the purpose of his preaching: "to make all men see what is the fellowship of the mystery, which from the beginning of the world hath been hid *in God*" (v. 9, emphasis added).

In other words, this work of God's grace, the gospel that Paul was given to proclaim, is that which reveals God's covenantal life. It reveals God's covenantal life as that life of unspeakable joy in the bond of fellowship and love. That which belongs to God himself from eternity within his own triune being he has been pleased to reveal by taking a people *in* Christ into his own household, into the fellowship of his life and love.

The inspired apostle proclaimed that gospel even with his prayer:

17. That Christ may dwell in your hearts by faith; that ye, being rooted and grounded in love,
18. May be able to comprehend with all saints what is the breadth, and length, and depth, and height;
19. And to know the love of Christ, which passeth knowledge, that ye might be filled with all the fullness of God. (Eph. 3:17–19)

What follows in chapters 4 through 6 is what the apostle speaks of as "walk[ing] worthy of the vocation wherewith ye are called" (Eph. 4:1). It is to bring to expression in this world the fellowship of that covenantal relationship with God into which *you* have been taken.

To live in God's covenant, to be partakers of that life of God's fellowship and love as members of his household, comes to expression especially in his family, the church. The apostle in chapters 4 and 5 demonstrates how that covenantal life comes to expression in the midst of the church—a church, mind you, made up of sinful people who still struggle with the effects of sin and with the old man of sin, even as redeemed children of God. How can that be done? Only by Christ's life coming to expression in us, his Holy Spirit applying the gospel to our hearts and minds.

For us to bring to expression the joy of life in God's covenant, we have to be living in the consciousness of the life that is ours in Christ Jesus, laying hold of him by faith. The same is true in the narrower relationships of life, including marriage.

The apostle does not suddenly enter a dissertation on marriage in this fifth chapter. There is no disconnect. He is continuing his contemplation and exposition of the mystery. In the immediate context of this section on marriage, we find the apostle expressing that life in terms of "giving thanks always for all things unto God and the Father in the name of our Lord Jesus Christ" (Eph. 5:20). Lives of thankfulness flow from the *mystery*, the wonder of our fellowship with God in Jesus Christ.

What a privileged place God has given us to be members of the bride of Christ! What a great privilege to live in the fellowship of God's loving embrace—especially when we know from *what* he saved us. The wonder of the mystery is seen exactly there. The mystery is not just the marriage of Christ and the church, as amazing as that is. But the mystery is great because of what it took for that union to be established. Jesus *gave himself* for us! He gave up his glory, the glory as of the only begotten of the Father, and became a servant. He came in our likeness, humbling himself even to the death of the cross, to cleanse us and to take us as his bride.

Do you see why the apostle speaks of that relationship between Christ and his church as a *mega*-mystery? And this is what marriage is to reflect! What a great privilege!

A Profound Calling

But what a profound calling! In married life, husbands and wives are to reflect the great mystery, the joyful life of fellowship and love between Christ and his bride.

The way you do that, says the apostle, is by "submitting yourselves one to another in the fear of God" (Eph. 5:21). That is what it is to reflect the life of Christ in you and the love of Christ for you. That is what it is to express our thankfulness to God and the Father in the name of our Lord Jesus Christ.

Such a relationship involves a tremendous amount of work, an incalculable number of acts of giving, expressions of love, and efforts to change—all reflecting the relationship between Christ and the church.

So true is this that if you are looking for a spouse who does not demand a lot of attention, who will not require significant change and spiritual growth, someone really "low maintenance"—to use a worldly expression—then your expectation of your spouse (or future spouse) is not only unrealistic but unbiblical. Such unbiblical idealism will prevent you from giving in a way that is necessary to reflect the relationship between Christ and the church. That is because such an unbiblical perspective fails to take into account the sinfulness of our sin, the weakness of our human nature, and the tremendous sacrifice and exercise of love required to reflect the love of Christ toward his church and the church's faithful giving in gratitude to her bridegroom, a giving that is expressed in a life of true conversion. That is the reality that our marriages must reflect.

It must not be forgotten, every man and every woman who enters marriage is broken by sin. That means, by the very nature of sin, they are self-centered. That again emphasizes the critical importance of marrying only in the Lord. The life of Christ must be present in us by faith in order for us to deal with the sins of our natures. But that also means that marriage is not a matter of looking for someone who accepts us as we are and who will fulfill all our desires. Since when did we seek Christ? He sought us! Since when did the church, Christ's bride, expect him to accept her as she was and to give her everything she desired? Where do you read that in the Bible?!

What we read in the context of Ephesians 5 is that Christ had to give himself for her, "that he might sanctify and cleanse it with the washing of water by the word, that he might present it to himself a glorious church, not having spot, or wrinkle, or any such thing; but that it should be holy and without blemish" (vv. 26–27). The inescapable implication is that his bride was filthy, nothing to look at in herself. That she would be made beautiful would be entirely his work, the exercise of his love.

As a husband, you are not to expect your wife to do all the work in making herself beautiful for you. We are not talking about something so superficial as her putting on her makeup. For your wife to be beautiful, to be the joy of your life, you must love her *even as Christ* loves his bride. You must *serve* her, *give* yourself to her, as the exercise of that love. That is your work, your godly service.

That does not take away your headship, the exercise of your leadership. But it radically changes the expression of that headship.

In the earlier chapters of this epistle, Paul had explained Christ's relationship to us from the viewpoint of Christ fulfilling God's purpose in forming us to the praise of his glory. We who were dead in sin—I'm speaking now of Christ's bride—have been quickened, made alive together with Christ, created *in* Christ Jesus unto good works. We live, in other words, to glorify our Redeemer! We live, according to Ephesians 4:20–24, putting off the old man, which is corrupt according to the deceitful lusts, and putting on the new man. That is true conversion, a change of mind and walk.

Whether husband or wife, each has as his or her calling to live for the other, to love, to give even sacrificially, in that covenantal relationship. To do that is to reflect the relationship of Christ and the church, the great mystery. That profound calling not only recognizes the mystery of the gospel, but knows the power of that gospel in our own lives. It sees the pattern for marriage given us in the relationship between Christ and the church.

Then, to submit to Christ not only comes to expression in repenting and believing the gospel. But to submit to him comes to daily expression in submitting also to one another, in seeking each other's spiritual welfare, in assisting each other on the way to heaven. As husbands and wives, we do not live for ourselves, but for each other. That is the most difficult aspect of our calling. But that is the radical change wrought by the Spirit of Christ in us when he raised us up and made us sit together in heavenly places in Christ Jesus.

A Blessed Relationship

By this change alone can we understand marriage as a blessed relationship.

It is by God's grace revealed in Christ Jesus that you and I know the joy of the Christian life. That joy is the fruit of grace. By grace alone, not for anything in us, God looked upon us in love from eternity. This is to say, he saw us *in Christ*, and never apart from him. By grace alone, God sent his Son to take us as his bride. By grace Christ pursued us, willing to lay down his life for us to redeem us from the bondage of guilt and sin and death that ensnared us and covered us with filth. Not only was he willing, but he humbled himself to the death of the cross. That is the price he willingly paid to make us his bride. By his Spirit and word, he poured his grace upon us, making us beautiful in his sight. By his grace he protects us, cares for us, provides for our every need. That is your bridegroom, Jesus Christ. Do you believe that?

That is the mystery. That is the wonder of the covenantal relationship into which God has taken us.

We deserve none of it. On the contrary. As Scripture makes

clear, by our sins we have repeatedly shown ourselves adulterers and adulteresses. God says in Jeremiah 3:1, "Thou hast played the harlot with many lovers." That is no made-up accusation of a jealous husband trying to manipulate his spouse. That is a fact. "Thou hast played the harlot with many lovers; yet return again unto me, saith the LORD." That is grace. The favor that we forfeited, he continues to pour upon us in faithfulness to that covenant he has established with his precious blood.

In the consciousness of this relationship he would have us live. He would fill our hearts with *love* for him. That is the blessed relationship of Christ and his bride. Is that relationship the center of your life, your thinking? That is the Christian life.

Marriage also, when lived in the expression of *this* marriage, is a blessed relationship. When you lay hold of the instruction of this text, you can see what a profound effect Christianity has on marriage. Put it in the historical context of Paul's writing, and you find a situation very similar to what we face today.

With an unbiblical view of marriage, such as is found, sadly, also within much of the church in our day, the joy of marriage as God intended is nowhere to be seen. When marriage is all about self, when marriage is sought in answer to the question, "What's in it for me?" marriage can only be a relationship the *opposite* of what God instituted it to be. Then marriage, even in the church, becomes scandalous, resulting in bitterness, unhappiness, and divorce.

So widespread is that corrupted view of marriage that even in the church people sometimes get married without really giving much thought to what marriage requires of them. They are attracted to each other. They want to be married. They think they are entering a certain partnership; but they never forsake the self-seeking. A man expects his spouse to answer to his desires, and the wife expects the same. But there is no spirit of humble submission to God, no reflection of what God requires of them in marriage, no contemplation of the great privilege and the profound calling that marriage entails, no readiness to humble themselves before each other, to confess sin, to admit wrongdoing. The proud notion of always being right presents an underlying antagonism and spirit of opposition. Many children grow up bearing the trial of seeing conflict where there should be unity.

What Paul preached was a relationship radically different, a relationship that *expects* joy, a relationship that reflects the blessedness of joy within God himself.

Think of the life of the Trinity. The three persons live in perfect unity. They do not manipulate each other. They do not use each other. Though three in persons, they are one. In revealing that joyful covenant, God sent his only begotten Son to take to himself a bride. He became one with her. His great love for her was revealed in becoming her servant, to draw her unto himself. And the bride, being cleansed and sanctified by the nurture and care of her husband, gives herself to him, loves him, longs to serve him in that love.

What a blessed relationship—to be expected by us, and to which we give ourselves in gratitude to the God who gave us a place in Christ's bride.

Don't forget, the Christian life can only be understood and lived as we understand and live out of the doctrine of the covenant, the great mystery. The same is true of marriage. When we understand the mystery, we understand the privilege of being able to reflect the mystery.

Mutual sacrifice, leading to mutual fulfillment—that is the reflection of the mega-mystery set before us in this text. That is the blessedness of a marriage lived in the consciousness of representing Christ and the church. That is marriage in which a husband and wife do not object to the principles and requirements of God's word, but submit to them and rejoice in them, and give thanks to God for the light of his word and the life that is ours in Christ Jesus. That is marriage that not only honors God, but testifies even before the world that life in Christ provides a joy unsurpassed by anything the world has to offer.

Chapter 10

GOD'S PURPOSE FOR US— LIVING JOYFULLY

Live joyfully with the wife whom thou lovest all the days of the life of thy vanity, which he hath given thee under the sun, all the days of thy vanity: for that is thy portion in this life, and in thy labour which thou takest under the sun.
—Ecclesiastes 9:9

When we speak about reasons to make sure that our marriages reflect the joy inherent in the covenantal life of fellowship with the living God, we must not forget that this is our *calling*.

Ecclesiastes 9:9 points to our calling in marriage, but also expresses God's purpose for us. The text comes from Solomon. It is given, of course, under the inspiration of the Holy Spirit. This is God's instruction for us. But it also expresses the wisdom to which Solomon himself had been led after many years of sorrow.

Ecclesiastes was written near the end of Solomon's life and reflects upon the vanity that he had pursued. It gives indication of the sorrow of repentance to which God had led him and the healthy reflection of one who was now able once again to discern spiritual things *spiritually*.

The purpose of Ecclesiastes is not merely to provide practical instruction; it is also the gospel of our Lord Jesus Christ. Solomon had been restored to life in fellowship with God. He had seen the need for the coming Messiah, the fulfillment of that type of which Solomon himself had been the failure. Solomon now knew the fellowship with God that could only come by the Prince of Peace promised in the gospel of our salvation. In repentance Solomon had laid hold of that promise by faith.

In that light Solomon reminds us that if life is to have meaning and direction, we must see more than that which is "under the sun." We must understand that which is heavenly and eternal, that which is revealed to us through Jesus Christ. In *him*, and only in him, can we live in joy during the "days of the life of thy vanity." That is true because only through the cross are we released from the bondage of sin and corruption. Only through the cross and our life in Christ do all things become our servants for Christ's sake. That is true also for marriage.

In the light of the gospel the preacher who is Solomon would teach us wisdom and lead us to the conclusion of the whole matter, which is, "Fear God, and keep his commandments" (Eccl. 12:13). The heart of this, as the Bible makes plain, is to love God with our whole being and our neighbor as ourselves. Standing in the promises of God that are in Christ Jesus, Solomon instructs us as to a proper biblical and spiritual perspective, giving us to see the treasure of God's grace in the midst of the vanity of an earthly perspective.

The Blessed Calling

Solomon, in Ecclesiastes 9:9, sets before us the blessed calling given by God himself. "Live joyfully with the wife whom thou lovest." The calling we are given here, the purpose of God expressed here for Christian marriage, presupposes something, even expects something. The blessed calling to live joyfully presupposes the *love* of a husband for his wife.

Solomon could not have written this without a deep pain coursing through the nerves of his own conscience. How he had violated this! How his own unrestrained lust had perverted the expression of marriage to which God had called him. What a failure as a type of Christ!

But Solomon, now knowing once again the love of God revealed in the promised Messiah, could write in the consciousness of the *true* marriage of which he himself was now partaker. So he speaks of "the wife whom thou lovest," expecting that husbands in a godly marriage *do* love their wives.

It is important that we understand this.

You remember that when Paul wrote in Ephesians 5 about the high calling of husbands and wives in marriage, he said, "Husbands, love your wives, even as Christ also loved the church, and gave himself for it" (v. 25). Paul exhorts us husbands to love our wives, that is, to *express* that love even as Christ expressed his love for the church.

Here, however, Solomon simply assumes that a godly husband loves his wife. That is expected in a man who is a child of God because true love is rooted in *God* and love for him. Love for the neighbor, also the neighbor within our own homes and marriages, is love that proceeds from and flows out of love for God. So true is this that John writes in his first epistle that for a man *not* to love his brother or sister or wife is to demonstrate that he hates God. He is "in darkness even until now" and "abideth in death" (1 John 2:9; 3:14).

A godly husband loves his wife because he has received her as a gift from the very hand of God. Thankfulness to God necessitates and motivates his love toward his wife. If you are a husband, is that true of you? Have you gotten beyond the infatuation that marks our flesh and draws our attention to the physical and outward appearance? It is true that a godly wife will care for her body for Christ's sake and because her body is a temple of the Holy Spirit. She will also look to her husband in that care for herself. The same ought to be true of any Christian man when it comes to his own body. But the love that Solomon expects of us and assumes in us who are children of the promise is a love that does not depend upon appearance. In fact, it is a love that continues to grow even when age robs a man's wife of her youthful appearance. It is love that receives her as God's gift, and for that reason it is an expression of thankfulness to God. It is love that focuses upon *Christ* and the love of God toward us *in* Christ, in whom all things are for our sakes.

This truth brings out another very important thing for us to see from this text. Notice that Solomon speaks here directly to the man, to the husband. When we look throughout Scripture for the instruction given to the wives, we find that there are no admonitions for the wives to love their husbands. Yes, the calling of a Christian is to love. That certainly applies within the home and to the wives. And we read in Titus that young women are to be *taught* to love their husbands. They must be taught how to bring that love to expression in the home and to their husbands. But the calling to love is explicitly given to the husband. Very important it is to consider that. Why is this true?

The reason love is *expected* and even *assumed* in this text as coming from the husband is expounded in the last part of Ephesians 5. Husbands are to love their wives because in this they are to reflect Christ's love for the church. The church did not first love Christ. Christ first loved her. Christ's love for his bride is so great, so intense, that it *creates* our love for him. His love is shed abroad in our hearts by his Holy Spirit, so that our love is our response to his love toward us.

Do you see what this text reveals to us from a practical point of view? A wife's love is to be generated by her husband's love for her. There have been many times in counseling couples going through marriage problems when I am sure the husband has thought, "The minister sides with my wife!" The husband will complain about his wife's bitterness, her coldness toward him: "She's always complaining, she's impossible!" And I ask, "How do you treat her? Are you her help, her support, her encouragement? Do you lead her in spiritual exercises? Do you listen carefully to what she says? Do you refrain from criticizing her? Do you set aside time to do things together and to give her a break from the children?" Questions like that can put a husband on the spot and make him feel very uncomfortable. That is not because I take any joy in finding fault in anyone's marriage. And invariably when there are marriage problems, there are enough sins committed by *both* husband and wife to compel a call to repentance to both of them. But those kinds of questions are necessary.

This text in the light of Ephesians makes clear that when a wife is not doing well in her marriage, the husband had better examine himself. When a husband is reflecting the love of Christ toward his bride, then his love for his wife will cultivate and nourish, even fuel, the love of his wife for him. I am not saying that there are no exceptions, especially when a man's wife shows herself unbelieving. But the exceptions would be rare. As a man goes, so goes his home. The wife and children reflect the godly headship of their husband and father—or the lack thereof. The wife and children reflect the *love* of a godly husband and father—or the lack thereof.

Love, after all, as is evident from Christ's love for us, is defined by *giving*. Christ loved the church and gave himself for it. So ought men to love their wives. That giving is not the giving of earthly things. To love your wife is not to shower her with material things. To love her is to give of *yourself*, to give her attention, to give her your time, your conversation, and, above all, your spiritual leadership. To love her is to nourish and cherish her, even as the Lord the church (Eph. 5:29). In the words of our text, it is to live with her, literally, "See the joy of life, with the wife whom thou lovest." You see that joy of life in no other way than by living with her, dwelling with her.

Here again we are given to see that marriage was created to be a human expression of the ultimate love relationship, our joyful union with Christ. Marriage signifies and is, for those who are married, a foretaste of the future blessedness of the kingdom of our Lord and Savior when we partake of the perfect fellowship of the marriage feast of the Lamb.

But that reminds us again that marriage is not the ultimate relationship. Also the blessed calling set before us in this text is a reminder of the *real* marriage of which we all must be partakers. It is impossible to bring to expression the joy to which we are called in this text if we attempt to put marriage on a higher level than our marriage to Christ. One great emphasis in premarital counseling must be the importance of husband and wife individually and together nurturing their own relationship with God in Jesus Christ. Without a growing, deeply fulfilling, and joyful relationship with Jesus Christ, your marriage *cannot be* what God would have it be.

Only when you realize personally and as a couple the glory of the relationship between Christ and his bride will you also realize the profound privilege and joy in being able to express and to reflect that relationship. That, after all, is the real marriage for which God has recreated us in Christ Jesus.

Singles too must remember this. The ultimate relationship is not earthly marriage. For all the emphasis that we place upon marriage and especially living marriage in the right way, we must not make an idol out of marriage. The Bible does not do that at all. The Bible shows how marriage serves the church and serves couples and serves as a reflection of that most important relationship to which God calls *all* his people. Just as married couples must rejoice in their marriage to Christ, if they are to live out of the joy of that lasting union, so those who are single must rejoice in their marriage to Christ, that they might live out of the joy of that relationship without being consumed by their dream of marriage or a sense of being unfulfilled in single life.

We all must remember that our marriage to Christ is the ultimate relationship. That truth underlies the important instruction in this text also for those who are married. Out of that love, out of the consciousness of the love of God for *you* in Christ Jesus, comes the blessedness of living joyfully with your wife.

The Fulfillment of That Calling

How is this calling fulfilled? This calling can only be fulfilled by *living with* her. That is really the heart of the admonition. Live joyfully *with* her.

We have considered already the significance of the one-flesh relationship God established in marriage. Solomon, to the great sorrow of his soul, knew the contrast. He did not dwell with his wife. He violated the unity of the one-flesh relationship. Now late in life he had turned from his sin in the godly sorrow of repentance. But he wrote this from a heartfelt desire that the children of God experience marriage and bring it to expression as God himself had instituted it. "Therefore shall a man leave his father and his mother, and shall cleave unto his wife: and they shall be one flesh" (Gen. 2:24).

One of the greatest hindrances to joyful marriage is the same self-centeredness that is so devastating to our relationship to God himself. Living joyfully with your wife calls you to selflessness. Our whole life is to be guided by the doctrines, the precepts, the principles, the perspective, and the promises of the word of God. We are so influenced by the world and the individualism and self-centeredness of our culture that we often do not even give any thought to our actions.

That is part of the gross misconception that often lies behind the claim of "Christian liberty." *I* want to do this. The fact that *God* owns us, including our bodies, the fact that we stand in relationship to others who might be damaged spiritually by our actions, perhaps drawn into sin themselves, does not even enter our minds when we are filled with the idolatry of self. Some men enter marriage that way. They are going to live as they please, seek what they please, do what they please, spend what they please, without regard to their wives. And then they wonder why there is no joy in marriage?

To live with and to give selflessly marks a husband's calling and lies at the heart of joyful marriage.

That does not come naturally. Solomon does not expect this of unbelievers. To see in the world men so caught up with business and pleasure that they have no time for their wives and children is no surprise. For years it was observed by Christian men who worked in factories that their fellow employees would go to the bar after work to "tip back a few" before they went home, and on payday often more than a few. Husbands in the church could not understand that because, living joyfully with their wives, they could not wait to get home to wife and children after a long day of work. Nothing would delay that. But the thinking of the world creeps into the church. Is your marriage such that nothing delays your getting home to your wife and to your calling as a husband in that relationship?

When I was working a 7:30 to 5:30 job in retail, I could not wait to get home to my wife and children at the end of the day. The thought of spending additional time after working hours—even ten or fifteen minutes—with the men I had already spent the whole day with (nice guys and all) would not even have entered my mind. I would get to work early in the morning and take only a short lunch break if I was busy. But I was not happy if a customer came in at the last minute and kept me from getting home.

But to live joyfully is more than just being at home. It is to participate in the joy of that relationship. It is to live as a happy, thankful husband. This is what the head of the home is to be like. That is, joy is to *dominate* his life as a husband and father. This is not to deny the fact that there are many sorrows and trials of our faith. This is not to ignore the sin that we must address as husbands and fathers. There are times when this expression of joy is going to be obscured by those things. But joy is to be the dominant characteristic of our lives. Our children need to see that. They need to hear how thankful to God we are for our wives. That ought to be expressed in our prayers.

What a tragedy, what a grievous sin on the part of husbands and wives, when children in the church grow up preferring to be any place but home, when instead of finding the home a place of joy and peace and happiness, the home is found a place of strife and anger and bitterness. That is not a covenantal home. That is a home where Christ is not present, a home where married couples are living in impenitent sin against God, and therefore where God has withdrawn himself.

The joy that is to mark our marriages is the same joy that should be our experience as those saved by Christ. In Jeremiah 33, the word of the Lord came to Jeremiah, speaking once again of the promise of salvation. That salvation is not just deliverance from the enemy nations and the bondage that God's people had to endure. But that salvation is found in this: "And I will cleanse them from all their iniquity, whereby they have sinned against me; and I will pardon all their iniquities, whereby they have sinned, and whereby they have transgressed against me" (v. 8). It was their sin, after all, that had robbed them of God's fellowship and the enjoyment of his love and favor. Salvation could only come through spiritual cleansing, the forgiveness of sins and reconciliation to God. That salvation, God says, will result in his people bearing a name of *joy*, joy that reflects the praise and honor of God our Savior. Jeremiah goes on to express that promise of Jehovah in terms of the joy that characterizes a bridegroom and his bride. "The voice of joy, and the voice of gladness, the voice of the bridegroom, and the voice of the bride, the voice of them that shall say, Praise the LORD of hosts: for the LORD is good; for his mercy endureth for ever: and of them that shall bring the sacrifice of praise into the house of the LORD" (Jer. 33:11).

The joy that characterizes our marriages is to be that which marks the blessedness of our salvation. That indicates, once again, that the joy of your marriage is going to correlate directly to the joy of your salvation. The husband or wife who does not live in the consciousness of Christ's sacrifice for us and the riches of his love toward us, the husband or wife who does not live in the joy of salvation, will not be able to live in the joy of marriage according to the calling of Ecclesiastes 9:9. But in the joy of our salvation, in the joy of *Christ*, we live our lives reflecting that joy—also in marriage. We do so in the same intimacy with which we have fellowship with our Redeemer.

When you stand before the gospel of your salvation, when you see the glory of Christ *for you*, when you are nurturing and growing in your spiritual life, also by the use of all the means of grace God gives us—not just the chief means of preaching and sacraments, but Bible studies and various aspects of the life of Christian fellowship—then you are living in the joy of fellowship with God in our Lord Jesus Christ.

In *that* joy you also bring to your own relationship the lessons learned and the joy experienced in that salvation. When the Lord, the husband of the church, reveals his grace, when he pours into the hearts of his own the blessedness of his forgiving love, when he gives us the experience of his grace as the victory over sin, when he speaks to us the word of his promise—what can we do but live in joy? "We will be glad and rejoice in thee" (Song of Sol. 1:4). That is the way it must be—also in our marriages.

The Reason God Would Have Us Live Joyfully

Having considered the blessed calling and the fulfillment of that calling, we must not fail to consider the reason God would have us live joyfully. Why? Solomon says, "For that is thy portion in this life" (Eccl. 9:9).

Think about this. Solomon throughout Ecclesiastes talks about the vanity of this earthly life. Some, for that reason, would make that life of vanity the antecedent to the expression, "That is thy portion in this life." But it is not. Solomon is setting forth a contrast here, a significant contrast. Everything about this life would rob us of joy. Therefore, when Solomon now gives the inspired command, "Live joyfully," he is calling us to reflect that which can only be ours in living relationship with Jesus Christ.

The portion that we are given in life is astounding in its beauty! The portion that we are given is not what we deserve. It is entirely a free gift of God's abounding grace. The portion that we deserve is what we taste in all the misery of this earthly sojourn, all the sin, all the sorrow, the death that surrounds us "all the days of the life of thy vanity." You see, we only have a short time to get this right! But God has given us *life*. He has given us life in the covenantal relationship that is ours in his own dear Son. He has given us life characterized by *joy*. I say again, that is a portion that not one of us deserved, the enjoyment of which none of us could have expected. John writes of this portion in 1 John 1 in terms of the fullness of joy, the fellowship that is ours with the Father and with his Son Jesus Christ, and therefore the fellowship that is ours also one with another as those who are *in* Christ, members of his bride.

But that fullness of joy that is ours, our portion in this life, is because Christ himself lives joyfully with us. He delights in us. He nourishes and cherishes us, rejoicing in our well-being. He gives himself for our sakes, bearing with our infirmities, turning us from our sins, filling our hearts with his love. In marriage he gives us the opportunity to reflect the joy of that relationship between Christ and his church. To all who are in Christ Jesus he gives the joy of his life and love. But in marriage he gives not only the privilege, but also the high calling to live joyfully. Yes, because of the sinfulness of our natures, that is also labor for us. Solomon speaks of that in the last clause of the text with reference to "thy labour." This requires effort. This demands *obedience*, the humble walk of a Christian.

Where we have been unfaithful, we must confess it before God *and* to our wives and children. "Confess your faults one to another" (James 5:16). That too belongs to the humble walk of a Christian.

But hear this word of God. He speaks it to our hearts, applying it by the power of his Holy Spirit: "Live joyfully." Live that way as a Christian, but in marriage, "Live joyfully with the wife whom thou lovest all the days of the life of thy vanity" (Eccl. 9:9). Live that way in thankfulness to God and to Christ our bridegroom. And know the blessing given to everyone who fears the Lord and walks in his ways.

Chapter 11

THE DIVINELY REQUIRED INTIMACY OF MARRIAGE

1. Now concerning the things whereof ye wrote unto me: It is good for a man not to touch a woman.
2. Nevertheless, to avoid fornication, let every man have his own wife, and let every woman have her own husband.
3. Let the husband render unto the wife due benevolence: and likewise also the wife unto the husband.
4. The wife hath not power of her own body, but the husband: and likewise also the husband hath not power of his own body, but the wife.
5. Defraud ye not one the other, except it be with consent for a time, that ye may give yourselves to fasting and prayer; and come together again, that Satan tempt you not for your incontinency.—1 Corinthians 7:1–5

When we search the Scriptures concerning living joyfully in marriage, we are repeatedly reminded that we stand before the wonder of the living marriage relationship between Christ and the church, the blessedness of the covenant that God has established with Christ and all who are united to him by a true and living faith.

The fact that God has also instituted marriage to reflect the glory of *the* marriage of Christ and the church gives not only a profound privilege to those who marry in the Lord, but an astounding calling. Only by our own union with Christ and the joyfulness of our life in him is found the possibility and expectation of living joyfully in marriage.

In 1 Corinthians 7:1–5 the inspired apostle sets forth God's purpose that the joy of intimacy be found also in the sexual relationship of a husband and his wife.

The Purpose of That Intimacy

To treat this text profitably for all, it is necessary to consider the purpose of the divinely required intimacy of marriage. To get to that purpose, we need to understand the apostle's approach in this seventh chapter of 1 Corinthians.

The focus in this text is the sexual relationship that God created and ordained exclusively for the expression of intimacy within the marriage relationship of husband and wife. The focus is *not* on instruction to those who are single to flee fornication. The apostle gave that instruction in the previous chapter, 1 Corinthians 6:18. He is not repeating that instruction here, and I am not treating that here either except indirectly in the positive development of this text.

It is important, however, to see the context and the reason why the apostle treats this particular subject in the context not of some marriage conference or instruction given in premarital counseling, but in a letter to be read to the entire congregation.

In chapter 7 we considered from 1 Corinthians 7:7–8 Paul's personal instruction to the unmarried and the glory of single life. We saw that God's way for each one of us is to be regarded by us as his *gift* for us and that which serves us according to God's perfect purpose. That is true of single life too. Single life, while constituting a trial for some, is not to be viewed simply as a cross to bear but as an opportunity to serve; even as in the capacity of marriage our calling is always one of service. But when we considered verses 7 and 8, I did not treat at that time the broader context of 1 Corinthians 7. It is necessary, though, to do that in our consideration of these first five verses.

In the first verse of this chapter, Paul refers to a letter that he had received from the saints at Corinth. There was correspondence between Paul and the church there, correspondence that began with the apostle confronting the church over some very serious weaknesses and sins, the reports of which had made their way to the apostle. Among those sins that plagued the church at Corinth and brought the chastening hand of God upon them was their refusal to address with Christian discipline sexual immorality among some within the church.

Bear in mind that this was a church primarily of Gentile converts, new believers, some of whom themselves had committed sexual sins, as is evident from chapter 6:11. Perhaps their own past made them hesitant to address others who were ensnared in those sins. Regardless of the reason, they had failed to glorify God and to maintain the necessary holiness of the church by overlooking and refusing to address in a biblical way sexual immorality among members in the church. Paul had to address those sins. He had to address them pointedly, in a way that his audience would be unable to escape the necessary instruction. So he had written to them in a previous epistle, we are told in chapter 5:9.

In the chapter before us, we find in verse 1 that Paul had received a response from the Corinthians. In that response they brought questions to the apostle about several matters over which there was confusion and probably some division, as well as other interest among God's people.

Paul writes, "Now concerning the things whereof ye wrote unto me" (7:1). If you study the rest of 1 Corinthians, you will find that there are several sections beginning here in chapter 7 that are introduced by this expression, "Now concerning." Paul is answering the questions they had raised. He does that here. He begins another section in verse 25. In chapter 8:1, he addresses a question they had raised concerning things offered to idols. In chapter 12:1, he responds concerning spiritual gifts. He responds to other questions in chapter 16. In each case, Paul states the subject that they had raised and to which he responds. That fact and additional examination of the Greek language sheds a little different light on this first verse.

When you look at verse 1 of chapter 7 and consider that expression, "It is good for a man not to touch a woman," while it is easy to consider that statement as *Paul's* response to a question they had raised, the statement is actually one of the things that the Corinthians have raised in their letter to Paul. The apostle is restating the position set forth in *their* letter to him.[1] It is similar to what Jesus did in his sermon on the mount, when he repeatedly said, "It hath been said," and followed it by, "But I say unto you."

There were those in Corinth who, having previously received Paul's instruction forbidding fornication, that is, all forms of sexual sin, concluded that it is *good* morally that any man abstain from touching a woman. There ought not be any physical contact between male and female. For a man to touch a woman is immoral. So far did they take this that the term for *man* in this first verse is a general term speaking of any man, including husbands. They were putting celibacy on a plane marked by *holiness unto the Lord* and saying any physical contact between male and female is sinful.

Here is another example of the error that often mars the beauty of the church and of the truth—the error of extremism. There is always the danger of falling away from the balanced view of the Christian life set forth in Scripture, marked by the joy of living in the fellowship of God's covenantal life. Some stray by attempting

---

1   A far more extensive exegetical treatment of and support for this position is found in David E. Garland, *1 Corinthians: Baker Exegetical Commentary on the New Testament* (Grand Rapids, MI: Baker Academic, 2003), 247–54.

to justify a walk in sin. Others are reactionary and would establish laws for their fellow Christians that have no basis in the truth of the word of God. The danger is falling off the balance beam either into licentiousness or into legalism.

In Corinth there were those who created a new category of sin, namely, that any man, including husbands, touch a woman, even if that woman be a man's own wife. Perhaps some would acknowledge the allowance of sexual relations within marriage for the purpose of childbearing. But any relations that would involve the touching of male and female, leading to the consummation of sexual relations, is wrong. This type of thinking would lead to that which the apostle would have to address some years later in 1 Timothy 4 concerning those who departed from the faith, giving heed to doctrines of devils, among which was "forbidding to marry" (4:3).

So here in 1 Corinthians 7, after having affirmed the *sanctity* of marriage in the preceding chapter and the need for and wonder of spiritual cleansing in Christ Jesus for those who had fallen, as well as setting forth the calling for all within the church to "flee fornication," Paul turns to a positive setting forth of the truth of marriage, sexual relations, and the gift of single life and subjects related to these issues. He would show the balanced perspective of the Christian life. He restates what at least some of the Corinthians had included as their perspective in their letter to him, and then he begins his correction in verse 2 by putting his hand out in the universal symbol of STOP and saying "But" or as our English translation has it, "Nevertheless." Not only has God ordained the sexual relationship exclusively for the marriage union of husband and wife, but there is a divinely *required* purpose in that intimacy.

First, let it be clearly understood that Paul is indeed speaking in these verses of the intimacy of the sexual relationship, what might be referred to as the act of marriage. The language he uses is not the crass language taken from the gutter of our fallen culture. We Christians are not to use vulgarities to speak of the beautiful, God-created sexual relationship. Paul speaks with unmistakable clarity about sex in marriage. But he uses terms that convey its *beauty*, its intimacy.

That is consistent with the whole Bible's presentation of this subject. The Bible does not view the sexual relationship with shame—when that relationship is confined, as is God's purpose, to marriage. Not only did God create the sexual relationship for a husband and wife as belonging to their good creation, not only did he give that to marriage before the fall, but we are familiar with Hebrews 13:4: "Marriage is honourable in all, and the bed undefiled: but whoremongers and adulterers God will judge."

The Bible in many passages speaks of the beauty of God's gift of sexual relations within holy marriage. But because of the beauty, the language the Bible uses to instruct us concerning this relationship is language that can be used in any company, including children. So Paul speaks of that intimacy of the act of marriage and says that it is *required* within marriage. Contrary to those who would view it as objectionable, or something only for the purpose of childbearing, it is *required* within the sanctified union of marriage. "Let every man have his own wife, and let every woman have her own husband" (1 Cor. 7:2).

We see from this text that the divinely required purpose for the act of marriage is for more than childbearing.

That childbearing is in part God's purpose in giving husbands and wives the sexual relationship is evident from the very institution of marriage in the beginning. In establishing the first marriage, God gave the charge, "Be fruitful, and multiply" (Gen. 1:28). That itself demonstrates the folly of the attempts being made today to redefine marriage. Two men cannot be fruitful and multiply, nor can two women. The ability to be fruitful and multiply, which characterizes marriage as instituted by God from the beginning, clearly confines marriage to the union of male and female. But the calling to be fruitful and multiply, the fulfillment of which is entirely subject to God's own will and providence for every marriage, makes clear that the sexual aspect of marriage is for the purpose of childbearing, and more particularly for the gathering of God's church in the generations of believers. We must view that obligation seriously and with sanctified understanding. To prevent the bringing forth of children for selfish motivations is a grievous violation of God's marriage ordinance.

What the apostle, however, makes clear in these opening verses of 1 Corinthians 7 is the fact that childbearing is not the *only* purpose for the act of marriage. That exclusive act, confined to marriage, also serves the sexual nature and desires that God gave man and woman. "To avoid fornication, let every man have his own wife, and let every woman have her own husband" (v. 2).

Notice, Paul is not saying every man must marry. In the following verses he addresses those who have the proper gift of God not to marry. There are also those who may not feel they have that proper gift, but for whom God in his wise providence withholds marriage and therefore promises grace sufficient to live in single life.

Nor is the emphasis of the text on instruction to young people to marry. It is true, that may be derived from this text. The liturgical form that we use in a wedding ceremony is not incorrect when referring to this text as a reason for young men and women to enter into the marriage state, "that each of them, avoiding all uncleanness and evil lusts, may live with a good and quiet conscience."[2] Young adults who carry on relationships for lengthy periods of time, without establishing that relationship upon the institution of holy marriage, place their souls in great danger. The sexual aspect of a person's makeup, as we already mentioned and as the Bible clearly teaches, is not something shameful or dirty. But it is very real. And

---

2   Form for the Confirmation of Marriage, in *Confessions and Church Order*, 307.

it belongs solely within the marriage bond. The physical desires that are so strong in youth are placed there by God himself. But they also are affected by sin and in many of us are areas of great weakness. It is in recognition of that fact that marriage becomes urgent for the young man and young woman whom God has brought together and made clear that they belong together as one in the Lord.

But we must not have the idea that the primary purpose of marriage is to flee lust. Even our marriage form states this matter as the third of three reasons why God has instituted marriage.[3] The fact is, simply urging people to get married will not solve the problem of sexual sins, nor the temptation to fornication. The purpose of marriage is far more glorious, as we have seen. The calling to flee fornication is a calling to maintain the glory of the marriage relationship, and not to defile it.

But the text before us speaks to the calling of husbands and wives, those who are already married. Paul rejects the error that it is holier, even in marriage, not to have sex. He says that to avoid sexual sin, every married man and every married woman is to express with his or her spouse the intimacy of their union by regular sexual relations. They are to do so to avoid falling into the temptation of sexual sin and violating that one-flesh relationship of marriage.

Sexual sin in whatever form—which is the meaning of that term *porneia*, "fornication"—might involve entering an improper relationship with someone other than your spouse, or flooding your mind with pornography, or, as Jesus said, looking at another person with lust. Fornication is to be avoided by rejoicing *together* in the intimacy that God has given to marriage. This unique expression of

---

3 "The first reason is that each faithfully assist the other in all things that belong to this life and a better. Secondly. That they bring up the children which the Lord shall give them, in the true knowledge and fear of God, to his glory, and their salvation" (Form for the Confirmation of Marriage, in *Confessions and Church Order*, 306–7).

intimacy reflects the unique intimacy of the relationship between Christ and the church.

To be celibate in a marriage relationship, except it be for a brief, agreed-upon period of time, is a recipe for disaster.

The Expression of That Intimacy

This intimacy therefore is to be expressed in regular sexual relations of a husband and wife. Paul explains this in terms of commitment that each spouse is to have toward the other. Verse 3 speaks of that which is *due*. "Let the husband render unto the wife due benevolence: and likewise also the wife unto the husband."

Marriage involves us in a relationship of indebtedness one to another as husbands and wives. This is to say that if you examine yourself in your marriage and find yourself to be demanding and self-centered, expecting your spouse to give and give and give, then you had better understand that your perspective of marriage is corrupted and requires repentance. Marriage is a relationship of indebtedness toward your spouse, the same way in which the church is indebted to Christ and you and I as Christians owe him our very lives and all our thoughts and actions. So much is that true that the apostle says in verse 4, "The wife hath not power over her own body, but the husband."

Notice, the wife also has the same power and the same rights as the husband. She is owed the same debt. This passage turns upside down the idea that Paul was a male chauvinist who had little regard for women. In fact, this teaching that a wife has power over her husband's body was radical in that world that hardly acknowledged women. But Paul writes, "Likewise also the husband hath not power of his own body, but the wife" (v. 4).

Underlying the truth of these assertions by the apostle is the divine pronouncement of marriage by God himself in Genesis 2:24: "And they shall be one flesh," the profound nature of which union we considered in the second chapter of this book.

That the sexual relationship in marriage emphasizes that indebtedness is clear not only from the apostle speaking of it in terms of giving what is *due*, but from the fact that in verse 5 he warns us against *defrauding* one another. To refuse the payment of this debt, to fail to express the intimacy of the marriage relationship in this way, is to steal from one's spouse that which God has rightfully assigned to him or her in marriage. It is to steal from them the intimacy, the joy, the pleasure that belongs to them in the marriage relationship.

There are times in God's providence when he deprives us of the act of marriage. There are times when God himself reminds us that the essence of marriage is not in the sexual relationship. There are times, in other words, in every person's life when we know singleness. That is true not only before we are married, when marriage is God's will for us. That is true not only after the death of a spouse or when forsaken by a spouse in divorce. But there are times when illness deprives us of this intimacy and gives us a taste of singleness, or times when business travels take a man away for a brief period of time, or times when a wife has to travel to help family members in need.

But for a wife to use sex as a weapon to deprive her husband of this debt except as a reward for good behavior, for a husband to defraud his wife by withholding from her this expression of his love, is not only to dishonor one's spouse, but to sin against God. This expression of our intimacy in marriage is our duty, our debt, toward husband or wife.

The expression of that intimacy within the marriage union is also prescribed by God himself as a debt of *love*. It is prescribed in terms of giving one to another, which is to say that a good sexual relationship comes from an intimate relationship of love. Love is not lust. Let's not equate those two. Did you notice the peculiar language the apostle uses to describe the act of marriage? Again, he is clearly referring to the sexual relationship. Of that there can be no question. "Let the husband *render*," i.e., pay out or recompense, "unto the wife due benevolence" (v. 3). Benevolence is the act of giving to one in need, providing for the needy. Interesting too that the Greek word is a word that expresses *enthusiasm* in that gift. The idea is really one of giving from the heart, an expression of our love and care for the one in need.

What a powerful piece of instruction this is when it comes to the act of marriage! How contrary to our culture's view of sex as the satisfaction of personal pleasure and self-gratification. The Bible would say, "You miss the whole point! You rob sex of its glory, of its beauty!"

There is an expression of intimacy that God purposed in the act of marriage that sets the sexual relationship far above the copulation of animals. As those who are the redeemed in Christ, we need to remember the glorious place God has given us in the fellowship of his love! We need to remember that the act of marriage is glorious, is beautiful, only when it expresses that intimacy of the relationship between Christ and the church, established by an unspeakably beautiful act of self-denying love and the giving that brought that love to expression to us poor and needy sinners.

The Blessedness of That Intimacy

We need to understand the blessedness of this intimacy given to marriage. It is important to remember in this connection the broader picture.

The apostle is not setting forth here a complete doctrine of marriage or even of the sexual relationship that belongs to the marriage bond. He is addressing this issue that has arisen in the church at Corinth, namely, the corruption of the sexual relationship pertaining to marriage. The Holy Spirit knew that we would face the same sin in the twenty-first century, and in ever-increasing measure. For that reason this instruction of the inspired apostle was also preserved for us and for our children. But Paul is not establishing an idea that the heart of marriage is sex, nor that the only value of marriage is that it averts fornication. If we separate this passage from the rest of what the Bible teaches about marriage, we are going to have as perverted a view of marriage as did some of the Corinthians.

God gave the act of marriage in order that a husband and wife might together reflect the strong desire for intimate fellowship with God through Jesus Christ, and in order that they might experience the exclusive and intimate relationship *they* have as a reflection of that relationship between Christ and his bride.

We must understand the divinely instituted intimacy of marriage in the light of the rest of what we have considered of the Bible's teaching concerning marriage, and in light of the Song of Solomon, which so beautifully expresses the intimacy of Solomon's marriage as representing the marriage between Christ and the church, between the *greater than* Solomon and his bride. Marriage, also in this beautiful expression of intimacy, serves God's purpose to glorify himself by reflecting the glory of his own covenantal life and the intimacy of the fellowship and love that he bestows upon us who are his in Christ Jesus.

Thus in verse 5, the apostle gives a reason for a married couple to abstain from this expression of their intimacy for a time. It is to recognize that our relationship to our heavenly Father is still chief. As Paul will go on in this chapter to point out, even as we considered in verses 7 and 8, the beauty of single life is found in a wholehearted devotion to living in the intimacy of one's union with Christ. The same is true in married life, but not in the same way. There are a multitude of distractions. And there are many more trials. Even the expression of intimacy in the sexual relationship, given by God to marriage, is frequently defiled by our own sinfulness and by our own selfishness. Also in this, we husbands and wives must bring our relationships to the cross for cleansing and for sanctification.

In addition, there are times in our lives when particular trials or needs or sorrows press upon us and compel us to flee to our heavenly Father in fervent prayer.

There are times when God himself knows that our relationship to *him* needs strengthening, that the intimacy of our fellowship with him has been lacking. In such times he draws us to himself. But as important as that is for us and for our marriages, we are to recognize our union as husbands and wives even in that. We are to consent to the need to give ourselves to fellowship with God. We do that only "for a time" (v. 5). Abstinence from the act of marriage may bring you closer to God; but extend it too long, and it might also bring Satan closer to you.

Fundamental to our marriages is our intimate fellowship with Christ our Savior. There is no joy without that union with Christ. Without living in the consciousness of the wonder of your forgiveness, you will never be able to give in the way that a joyful marriage requires.

But when God has led you in the way of repentance to see the glory of your Redeemer, to recognize the beauty of your bridegroom, Jesus Christ, that joy will come to expression in your life. And when marriage is God's purpose for you, the intimate fellowship that you have with him is also to come to expression in your marriage. Our marriages are to reflect the mystery. May Christ's intimate expression of love for you be *your* joy.

Part 3

Dedicated to Expressing the Joy

Chapter 12

THE EXERCISE OF LOVE

For all the law is fulfilled in one word, even in this; Thou shalt love thy neighbour as thyself.—Galatians 5:14

The exercise of love is what I would consider the first essential, if we are dedicated to expressing the joy in marriage. The calling set before us in Galatians 5:14 is not limited to earthly marriage. Rather, it is the calling of the Christian. It is the calling of the Christian because—as I have emphasized—every Christian stands in a marriage relationship to Jesus Christ. We are all members of Christ's bride, of his flesh and of his bones. For that reason, as we treat in the following chapters what is involved in a dedication to living joyfully in marriage, you will see that the subjects we consider have broad application in the life of every Christian. Whether we consider the exercise of love, dying to self, the importance of forgiving one another, or other essentials to living joyfully in *marriage*, you will immediately recognize that such themes are also essentials to living joyfully *as Christians*.

The calling to love is so prevalent in Scripture that I could use any number of passages to develop this essential of living joyfully. Being the essence of the law, it defines the Christian life. John writes in his first epistle, in fact, that the lack of love is a sure sign of spiritual death. Not only does the Holy Spirit press this truth upon us in John's first epistle, but there is an entire chapter in the Bible, 1 Corinthians 13, that unfolds the way of love in the life of the Christian as the "excellent" way in which the life of Christ appears by his Spirit's work in the hearts of his people. In addition, Ephesians 5 calls the followers of God to walk in love, as Christ also has loved us (verses 1 and 2). But it goes on to apply that calling specifically to husbands in the latter part of that chapter, as we have seen in our consideration of the great mystery that marriage reflects, namely, the relationship between Christ and the church.

The Great Calling

You recognize the great calling set before us in Galatians 5:14 as the second part of the summary of the law given us by our Lord Christ. Contrary to the error of the Pharisees, who put all the focus on doing the letter of the law, including their own additions to the law, and upon the occasion of their tempting him to contradict the law of Moses, Jesus said, "Thou shalt love the Lord thy God with all thy heart, and with all thy soul, and with all thy mind. This is the first and great commandment. And the second is like unto it, Thou shalt love thy neighbour as thyself. On these two commandments hang all the law and the prophets" (Matt. 22:37–40). When the Pharisees would point to their works, to all that they had done, and to their supposedly wise dealings with the law of God, Jesus said in Luke 16:15, "Ye are they which justify yourselves before men; but God knoweth your hearts: for that which is highly esteemed among men is abomination in the sight of God."

If your *hearts* are right with God, proper Christian living will follow. And if your hearts are *not* right with God, if they are not filled with the love of God that also comes to expression toward the neighbor, everything you do is found abominable with God.

In the text before us, the emphasis falls upon that great commandment in its second part. "For all the law is fulfilled in

one word, even in this; Thou shalt love thy neighbor as thyself"
(Gal. 5:14).

I selected this text for consideration exactly because of its
breadth. This text does not focus simply on the husband's calling to
love his wife. The law of God presses upon every one of us. It presses
upon us as members of Christ's bride. It provides the standard by
which we may be sure that we *are* members of Christ's bride. But
the breadth of this calling is seen especially in the fact that the text
presses upon you to love your *neighbor* as yourself.

The Pharisees made clear that in their estimation they could
restrict the definition of the neighbor. The child of Abraham was
the neighbor. Some would restrict it further and claim that only
the child of Abraham who lived by the right standards was the
neighbor—and those standards, of course, were the self-determined
standards of the Pharisees.

Jesus, however, had made unmistakably clear that the concept
of the neighbor was far more broad, even uncomfortably broad, to
us. That neighbor is anyone with whom we live or who crosses the
pathway of our life, regardless of the person's beliefs, background, or
behavior. The way in which that love will be expressed is a different
question. But the calling to love your neighbor as yourself presses
upon every one of us without exception.

It is also true, however, that the closer God has linked us
together, the more this great command presses upon us and requires
that we bring to expression the love to which we are called. For that
reason, even though Jesus applies this commandment so broadly as
to require love even toward our enemies, the apostle John addresses
particularly those relationships much closer, those within the church.
"We know that we have passed from death unto life, because we love
the brethren. He that loveth not his brother abideth in death" (1
John 3:14). Or 1 John 4:10–11: "Herein is love, not that we loved
God, but that he loved us, and sent his Son to be the propitiation

for our sins. Beloved, if God so loved us, we ought also to love one another."

We all recognize that there is no neighbor closer than those within our own homes. And there is no neighbor so close as a wife to her husband, and a husband to his wife. We have many neighbors; but the neighbor we face most often is the one at home—a spouse, a child, parents, brothers and sisters. The calling is to *love* the neighbor, also that neighbor in our own home.

What is that love? Let's understand, we do not have the option to define love on our own terms.

There are different words for "love" in the Greek language, two of which are used in the New Testament. The one speaks of brotherly love, of having affection for someone. But there is another word that elevates the meaning of love to a concept far beyond human affection or feelings. This is the word the Bible always uses to express God's love. It is the term used to speak of God's love as an essential attribute of his being, that which is expressed within the triune God in the relationship of the three persons of that holy Trinity. It is also the term used to express God's love to *us* who are in Christ Jesus. It is the term used in Romans 5:8, "But God commendeth his love toward us, in that, while we were yet sinners, Christ died for us."

The same term is used in Ephesians 5:25 with application to marriage, particularly to the calling of the husbands: "Husbands, love your wives, even as Christ also loved the church, and gave himself for it." Notice that. Love is defined by *giving*. It is defined by giving that seeks the welfare of the object of that love. That is why 1 Corinthians 13:4–7 says, "Charity [and that is the word *agape*, this greatest love of all] suffereth long, and is kind; [love] envieth not; [love] vaunteth not itself," that is, does not brag about itself, "is not puffed up, doth not behave itself unseemly, seeketh not her own, is not easily provoked, thinketh no evil; rejoiceth not in iniquity, but rejoiceth in the truth; beareth all things, believeth all things, hopeth all things, endureth all things."

In Romans 13:9, after setting forth the second table of the law, the specific commandments that speak of our relationship to the neighbor, the inspired apostle Paul says that the summary of it is this: "Thou shalt love thy neighbour as thyself." Then follows what we read in verse 10, "Love worketh no ill to his neighbour." Think of that! "Love worketh no ill to his neighbor: therefore love is the fulfilling of the law" (v. 10). To do *only good*, only that which serves and strengthens the neighbor—that is love. How far short do we fall of that calling?!

Look at the characteristics of Christ's love toward his church, his bride. He did not dwell on her deficiencies. He did not focus on the negatives. Then he would certainly have cast her off. He focused on her needs, on what he would do to save her, to help her, to strengthen her. He loved her in spite of her natural ugliness, in spite of her deficiencies. He saw even her sins as that which was to be corrected by his own careful word. He would wash her; he would cleanse her. He would give his *life* for her!

Read the Bible. See how Jehovah's love for his people comes to expression. That is the whole Bible! Throughout the Bible you find him doing whatever it takes to save his church, the object of his love. He chose her to be special. She *was not* special. There was nothing in her that distinguished her from any other human beings. But he would *make* her special. He would do her good. He would strengthen her, protect her, see her as he would have her be, rather than letting her own faults consume her. He could not let that happen! Not when he loved her. He desired that she be perfect. And he would not be satisfied until he had finished his own work in her. That is love.

That is the love that is required of you toward your wife, toward your husband, toward your fellow church member, toward your neighbor. That is the specific application to marriage, as we read in the last part of Ephesians 5. Christ would give his life for his church whom he loved. He would do so with a purpose: "That he might sanctify and cleanse it with the washing of water by the word, that he might present it to himself a glorious church, not having spot, or wrinkle, or any such thing; but that it should be holy and without blemish" (Eph. 5:26–27).

Christ seeks the transformation of his bride into that which is spiritually beautiful. That is the love he requires of us. We have a unique responsibility as Christians to seek each other's spiritual growth. That begins in the home.

Do not kid yourself into thinking that anything less fulfills this requirement. Love is defined by *this*, to do that which serves and strengthens, nothing less. This *only* is the fulfilling of the law.

The Absolute Necessity

The necessity of loving one another is absolute. There are no exceptions to this great calling, also now as we apply it to marriage.

It is important that we understand this. Everyone has weaknesses, and everyone has his or her own sinful nature. If that is what we are going to dwell on, we will not love but will show ourselves hateful and vindictive. This has been the destruction of many in the church. This has been the destruction of many marriages.

Our young adults and young people must understand that the man or woman whom you see *before* you are married is different from the man or woman you will see *after* you are married. That is why marriage calls for constant adjustments. That is true not only because we are always facing changes in our lives—marriage changes us, children change us, the trials and experiences of life change us, age brings change—all of which demand adjustments and working through those changes together. It is true, if you have a spiritually healthy relationship before marriage, you will see some of your differences, some of the flaws or challenges in your relationship. You will talk about them. And in talking, you will watch very carefully the kind of response that you receive. But the fact is, marriage brings out everything in your nature that you tried to hide. Every sinful aspect of your nature will be exposed to your spouse, and vice versa.

That brings up something very important for young people and young adults to realize. The fact is, when we are "in love," we also can be quite blind. That is why parents, who love and have a vested interest in the spiritual welfare of their children, are wise to discuss openly with their sons and daughters any relationship that could lead to marriage. Parents and young people ought to be communicating about *all* the children's relationships. But when young people think they are "in love," parents might see matters of concern to which their child is blind. Because they love their child, they will ask, "Have you talked about this? How is he or she going to deal with these circumstances? If he occasionally snaps at you, if he shows a lack of self-control or has anger issues, how do you think he is going to treat you when you are married and have no way out?" Young people must listen to the warnings of parents or friends, who may see matters of concern that the young person is unable or unwilling to see.

There will be sins and character flaws that you must address in marriage. When that "in love" phase passes, the things that did not seem very big will become much larger. That is why so many, within a rather short time after being married, throw up their arms and say, "I married a stranger! This is not going to work!" Not willing to put in the work of this labor of love, not knowing the love of Christ, they simply move on to someone else. You and I stand before the absolute necessity of love. That is our calling in the church. That is our calling in marriage.

What are the character traits that are going to come to expression in your marriage and in your relationships within the church?

Perhaps you are opinionated and abrasive, one whom people tend to tolerate rather than appreciate. Perhaps you tend to be demanding and selfish. Is that weakness one of being manipulative and sullen when you do not get your way? Are you undisciplined and sloppy in your work habits? Are you inclined to be fearful, one who dwells on the negatives? Perhaps you are a worrier, easily anxious. Maybe you are a perfectionist who not only finds it difficult to accept anything less of yourself, but who has little patience for others as well.

There are many, many flaws in us because of our being partakers of the fall of Adam. The closer we are in proximity to each other, the more those weaknesses and sins are going to be seen. They become inescapably evident in marriage. But no matter whether we apply this to marriage or to life within the church, the necessity of loving one another is absolute and inescapable.

According to the calling of the gospel, you have to make it work; which is to say, the love to which you are called not only begins *before* marriage, but must continue through your whole life.

Children and young people must be taught what love is. The greatest need for children is to see a father and mother who love each other for Christ's sake. They need to be taught what love is by both seeing it come to expression in the relationship of their parents and also by being themselves the objects of that love by their parents. They need to be taught what love is by being led to Christ. They need to be shown him who loved us while we were yet sinners, who loved us by *giving* himself for us and by continuing to give himself *to* us, seeking our purification and salvation without fail. They need to see Jesus loving us enough not to give up on us, but leading us to repentance, giving us a sorrow for the sin we committed against God, and empowering us by his Holy Spirit to turn from our sins and to live to his glory.

That means these things must be seen in our marriages. What

will our children know about love if all they see is the bickering and demanding, "I don't have to change! *You* change!" What will they ever know about true love if they see their father sin repeatedly but never hear him confess it and say, "I am sorry; I have sinned"? What if all they sense in the home is rejection? Then all they see is the wickedness of our sinful pride and the hardness of our sinful hearts.

In our calling to love the neighbor in marriage, we husbands must look upon our wives in the consciousness of how Christ has looked upon us. Those weaknesses that we come to observe *after* we are married must be looked upon as opportunities to show the love of Christ who always seeks to strengthen, to sanctify us.

Here is where the calling to love her husband also presses upon the wife. Notice, this calling of Galatians 5:14 comes to everyone. In Ephesians 5:25, the calling is given to husbands, "Love your wives." In that chapter we are told that marriage reflects the relationship of Christ and the church, so that wives are to reflect the church's submission to Christ. But the figure of wives representing the church and husbands representing Christ is limited by the vast chasm of our own sinfulness. The husband-wife relationship is *like* that of Christ and the church. It is *not* identical.

The marriage relationship is constantly to be brought into conformity to that glorious relationship of Christ and his bride. Our lives are to be lived in the consciousness of that unbreakable covenantal union. But we must so live, and our lives and marriages must be brought into conformity to that glorious relationship, because we are constantly dealing with our own sinfulness.

Our lives, our relationships, must be sanctified. That work of the Holy Spirit through the word is a work he performs also through the means of relationships, of helping and encouraging one another. From this point of view, it is important that wives also love their husbands. Husbands *and* wives are both members of Christ's bride, who needed to be cleansed. So in marriage, it is not only wives who need to be nourished and cherished, cleansed and sanctified, by their husbands. Husbands need that same change. It is called repentance. It is called the need for spiritual growth and sanctification. It is called the need to be encouraged in godliness.

In that way wives also stand before this great calling as an absolute necessity. Wives also need to give themselves for the spiritual strength of their husbands. Their love is to come to expression by serving him with exactly that goal in mind, to see him strengthened as a man of God. You do not do that by nagging, by continual faultfinding and complaining. The Bible often warns against counterproductive speech. Speech that simply tears down is the opposite of what love compels us to do, namely, to speak the truth in love. Cutting words stir up anger. But wives win their husbands by their sacrificial behavior and kind and loving words.

Ephesians 4:15 says that "speaking the truth in love, [we] may grow up into him in all things, which is the head, even Christ." Love compels us to work toward pleasing each other in the Lord, seeking one another's spiritual growth and strength, and helping each other overcome our weaknesses.

The Only Possibility

You and I can only exercise such love, whether in the midst of the church or in our marriages, if the Spirit of Christ dwells in us. That is evident when you look at Galatians 5:14 in the light of the verses that follow.

"For all the law is fulfilled in one word, even in this; Thou shalt love thy neighbour as thyself." Now read the next two verses: "But if ye bite and devour one another, take heed that ye be not consumed one of another. This I say then, Walk in the Spirit, and ye shall not fulfil the lust of the flesh" (vv. 15–16). Walk in the Spirit! That is the only possibility for loving one another.

That is why, I say again, your spiritual life is the cellular foundation, as it were, for the health of your marriage and for the health of your relationships in the church, Christ's bride. To say to the unbeliever, "You have to love your neighbor; you have to love your spouse," is only to point to the hopelessness of his human condition. He is *incapable.*

The apostle is addressing those who belong to Jesus Christ, those in whom the love of God is shed abroad in their hearts by the Holy Spirit who is given unto us (Rom. 5:5). One of the ways we show that the Spirit dwells in us is that husbands love their wives, wives love their husbands, and we *all* love the members of Christ's bride. For in doing so we reflect the relationship of Christ and the church.

That means that to love one another, also within marriage, we must know the truth about the relationship of Christ to his church, and of the church to Christ.

Here again we see the importance of knowing God and his truth. Ephesians 5:1–2 tells us, "Be ye therefore followers," that is, *imitators,* "of God as dear children: and walk in love, as Christ also hath loved us, and hath given himself for us an offering and a sacrifice to God for a sweetsmelling savour." If you are going to be an imitator of God, you must know God. He cannot be a god of your own imagination. Because he is God, absolutely set apart as the Holy One, it is impossible for you to know him except he makes himself known to you. He does that in his word, by his gospel. He reveals himself as the covenantal God, the God of relationship. If you are going to be an imitator, you must know him that way.

Furthermore, you must know him *intimately.* You must know him in love, "as dear children" know their father who counts them dear and who loves them. Some do not have an earthly father like that; they never did. That is all right. God is more than any earthly father. But you must know him for who he is. And you must know him in *that* intimacy.

Furthermore, to be an imitator of him, the text states explicitly, is to walk in love, "as Christ also hath loved us." This is to say, "We must know Jesus." We must know his relationship to his bride. We must know the grace by which that relationship was established.

Do not let anyone tell you that the doctrine of God and of his Christ is not important. The exercise of love depends upon this knowledge. First John 4:9–11 says,

9. In this was manifested the love of God toward us, because that God sent his only begotten Son into the world, that we might live through him.
10. Herein is love, not that we loved God, but that he loved us, and sent his Son to be the propitiation for our sins.
11. Beloved, if God so loved us, we ought also to love one another.

Our love must be sacrificial, a love that gives for the benefit of the other. Husbands, love your wives like that; wives, love your husbands in that way.

And do not forget, what we are told about that relationship of Christ and his church applies to the calling of every one of us. Do you believe? Are you a child of God? Christ is your husband. According to Romans 7:4, we are married to him. To live in that consciousness is the heart of the Christian life, essential also to living joyfully in marriage.

Chapter 13

DYING TO SELF

2. Fulfil ye my joy, that ye be likeminded, having the same love, being of one accord, of one mind.
3. Let nothing be done through strife or vainglory; but in lowliness of mind let each esteem other better than themselves.
4. Look not every man on his own things, but every man also on the things of others.
5. Let this mind be in you, which was also in Christ Jesus.— Philippians 2:2–5

As the exercise of love is essential to living joyfully as a Christian, so it is essential to living joyfully in marriage. The calling to love—and love is a calling, not merely a feeling—presses upon every one of us. There is joy in marriage and family life only in the way of love, because only in that way do we reflect the very life of God himself and the covenantal fellowship that he enjoys with his people in Christ Jesus.

The second matter to consider in a dedication to expressing the joy of holy marriage necessarily follows the first. When love is an act of giving, even sacrificially, and doing that which serves and strengthens the neighbor, there is necessarily involved a setting aside of self and selfish motivations in order to seek the good of the object of our love.

The Understood Necessity

As we stand before Philippians 2:2–5, we immediately understand the need for this admonition. The fallen human nature with which we are born is selfish and self-focused. We are all idolaters of self. That is our very nature.

Parents might hold their little baby in their arms, and that baby will be a picture of contentment so long as he has what he wants and so long as all the attention is given him. But throw a sibling into the mix, or watch that child get just old enough to be able to get around and then set another child with him in front of a variety of toys, and they do not just pick up separate toys and play nicely together, do they? They have to have the same one. If they are old enough to verbalize it, they will scream what lies in the darkness of their hearts: "Mine!"

So the first lesson in life you have to teach a child, and that already in infancy, is that the world does not revolve around him. A child will wear his mother to a frazzle if the mother always responds to that demand for attention. That child, well-fed and just recently changed, who simply cries for attention at night must be left to cry. The lesson begins already at that very young age and must continue to be taught with persistence—because selfishness certainly persists. This life is not about me, myself, and I.

This life is about *us* collectively, as together we serve the living God our Creator. The purpose of God for us, as is evident from the first two verses of Philippians 2, is that we be like-minded, having the same love, being of one accord, of one mind. In fact, in verse 2, the Holy Spirit uses a striking word to unveil the beauty of the oneness that ought to characterize us. I refer to the word translated in our English version by the expression *of one accord*. It is a word that speaks quite literally of a symphony of souls. There is to be that same harmonious blending of our souls that is found in the music of an accomplished symphony. The oneness that ought to characterize a husband and wife in marriage, and that flows from the expression of self-denying love, is the oneness that also ought to characterize our families and the church family.

But our natural selfishness tears at the fabric of that unity. The orchestra is playing that symphony in beautiful harmony, when suddenly selfishness sounds forth the noise of an intruding duck call. Think about it. Marriage troubles do not arise from husband and wife being too selfless, too humble, do they? Troubles do not arise from being too loving, too giving, do they? After all, 1 Corinthians 13:5 tells us that love "seeketh not her own." Troubles arise from the noise of *self* breaking the quietness of peace and joy. When there is trouble at home, the first thing we have to look at in the light of God's word is self. How am I contributing to what is not right here? Of what sins must I repent? What can I do to correct this?

It is important for us to understand this and to live with an acute awareness of personal responsibility and our own inclination to the idolatry of self.

There has been a fundamental shift in thinking concerning marriage through the years. Especially in the past two generations, that shift has become a landslide. The Christian view of marriage, which holds marriage as reflecting the covenantal relationship of sacrificial giving and nurture and love of Christ for his church and the church in response to Christ, has been replaced by a view reflective of what Paul warned would be characteristic of the perilous times of the last days, when "men would be lovers of their own selves" (2 Tim. 3:2). "What's in it for me?" The gratification of the individual marriage parties is the dominant thought concerning marriage today.[1]

That way of thinking has been fueled also by the sexualized culture in which we live and the influence of pornography that has

---

1   Demonstrated clearly by John Witte Jr. in his book *From Sacrament to Contract: Marriage, Religion, and Law in the Western Tradition* (Louisville: John Knox Press, 1997), 194–98.

affected so many even in the church, not just men either, but women as well. The philosophy of hedonism, life being about self-gratification, self-satisfaction, has poisoned many marriages. Thus, instead of being a relationship seeking the welfare of each other and the joy of covenantal fellowship, marriage has become in the minds of most a private arrangement for personal satisfaction. Where marriage is supposed to be about *us*, it has now become about *me*.

This thought that permeates our culture readily influences our perspective as well, because it is a thought rooted in our sinful hearts. It is seen, for example, in the irritability or resentment we might express when our spouse states the desire that we change something about ourselves or our behavior. "You should be willing to take me as I am!" "Quit trying to change me!" Instead of considering what our spouse is telling us and why that change might not only be desirable, but necessary for *God's* glory, it is all about self. That self-centeredness is deeply rooted in our own sinful nature and in the pride of our own hearts.

That truth is brought out in Philippians 2:3–5. The text confronts our self-centeredness when it instructs us, "Let nothing be done through...vainglory" (v. 3). The term *vainglory* speaks of the vanity of pride and conceit. You recognize, then, that the term speaks of the opposite of humility. It speaks of "my way or the highway," ruling by opinion rather than by humble subjection to the word of God. When you throw that self-centered attitude into a marriage relationship, you rob yourself of any possibility of joy in that relationship.

Paul speaks more broadly than just the marriage relationship. The same is true in the church. Self-centeredness is not some vague concept. It comes to expression in many different ways. The irritability that sometimes characterizes us, our impatience, the lack of kindness in speech and carefulness in judgment, the refusal to let go of past hurts—all those things really come down to our own self-centeredness. We have such a high view of ourselves—the vain-glory Paul warns against—that we tend to be hyper-sensitive, easily offended, while blind to our own faults. The result is anger and self-pity. These things will consume any relationship, whether marriage, friendships, or relationships in a congregation.

But not only are we warned against the self-centeredness expressed by the concept *vainglory*. We must also recognize that to live selfishly is to bring strife to a relationship. Verse 3 uses that word *strife*: "Let nothing be done through strife or vainglory."

The word translated *strife* speaks of selfish ambition corrupting a positive virtue. It speaks of one who is highly motivated. To be highly motivated in the service of God and to his glory is a positive virtue. Would that we were all highly motivated to serve God always, to live in the light of his precepts! After all, as we saw in 1 John 5:2, "By this we know that we love the children of God, when we love God, and keep his commandments."

That word *strife* speaks of the one who is highly motivated, but who uses that virtue in self-seeking. In fact, to give some indication of what a negative concept *strife* is, it is a word used to describe the politician who, unchecked by moral inhibitions, contends for personal success at the expense of what is right. He will do whatever it takes to be re-elected, jockeying for position, deceiving, and scheming to come out on top. Is that what your marriage would be like? You can see how devastating that is to a relationship in which two are to live as one. When we live unto self, we only hurt ourselves. When we seek our own self-interests and live selfishly in our relationships, we hurt ourselves because we are living contrary to the way God calls us to live.

To put it clearly, we are living in rebellion against God when we are self-centered. If we are to live joyfully in marriage therefore, there has to be a dying to self. The same is true with our relationships in our families and in the church, the bride of Christ.

The Pressing Requirement

This necessary dying to self comes with specific requirements that press upon each one of us.

First, "let each esteem other better than themselves" (Phil. 2:3). How do you view each other? How am I to view you, and you me? "Let each esteem other better than themselves."

What does that mean? Clearly, God gives all of us different gifts. So what does this mean when a wife may be more gifted in many areas than her husband? Is she simply to ignore her own gifts and consider her husband better than her? Suppose the husband finds his wife to be more of a leader, a more decisive decision-maker. Is he to relinquish his role as the head of the home? You can immediately sense that such an interpretation of this text not only would be unrealistic, but would contradict other Scripture. The husband may never relinquish the position God has entrusted to him as the head of the home; nor may the wife usurp that role, even when the husband has to make great effort, because of the weakness of his nature, in carrying on his calling.

In the church too, we are to recognize with thanksgiving the gifts that God has given us and use them to his glory, while at the same time rejoicing in the gifts God has given others and encouraging those who are less gifted. The Bible is full of instruction concerning those relationships. When the text tells us, "Let each esteem other better than themselves," it is telling us that when we look at each other, fellow Christians redeemed by the same blood of Jesus, we are to view the other as *superior* to ourselves. That is to say, "That person is worthy of my *service*."

Perhaps this is best illustrated by the Bible's account of some dissension among the disciples that came to expression at the last supper. Of all times, when the suffering of our Lord was beginning to press upon him, the very night when those sorrows would press out of him the bloody sweat in the garden of Gethsemane, Jesus' own disciples added to his sorrows by striving among themselves. We read of it in Luke 22. We learn in Mark 9 that they had carried on this dissension for some time. This was not a new squabble. But now, in the last night they would spend with their Lord, and at a time when you would think that there were plenty of other things to occupy their time and thoughts, we read in Luke 22:24 that there was strife among them. They disputed about which of them should be accounted the greatest.

The Bible, in all its realism, pointing us to the stark reality of the wretchedness of our own natures, would have us see that if Jesus' own disciples were caught up in such sin, in such self-centeredness and pride, how easy it must be for us to commit the same sins and to grieve the Holy Spirit.

Jesus confronted that sin, first by pointing to the world and the pride of prominence seen among the heathen. He then said, "But ye shall not be so: but he that is greatest among you, let him be as the younger; and he that is chief, as he that doth serve" (Luke 22:26). There must be a dying to self! Then Jesus pointed to himself: "For whether is greater, he that sitteth at meat, or he that serveth? is not he that sitteth at meat? but I am among you as he that serveth" (v. 27).

To regard the other as superior, to esteem the other better than ourselves, is to deem him or her worthy of service. It is to express a willingness to expend ourselves for the benefit of the other. The only way we will do that is by looking at one another in the light of the gospel and seeing one another in the light of God's grace. Then we are not criticizing one another and judging each other for every character weakness we can observe, but seeing the beauty instilled by the amazing grace of God in Jesus Christ.

When that is our calling toward our brothers and sisters in the church, how much more to that spouse with whom you are one flesh! No, this does not conflict with the husband's calling to exercise authority in the marriage relationship, no more than it conflicts with various authority relationships within the church. But it does define those relationships in a way radically different from how the world views such relationships. Christ points us to the fact that authority relationships involve service—service to God first of all, and then to those on whose behalf we exercise that authority.

In that light, then, we see in the fourth verse of Philippians 2 the second pressing requirement in this necessary dying to self, namely, "Look not every man on his own things, but every man also on the things of others."

You will remember that when it comes to the role of a wife, Ephesians 5:22 defines that role by one word, and not an easy word either. It is the word "submit." "Wives, submit yourselves unto your husbands, as unto the Lord." What is easily forgotten, however, is that just prior to spelling out the specific callings of wives and husbands, the apostle had been speaking more broadly of relationships within the church. He was speaking about the calling that every one of us bears as children of God. We are to be followers of him, that is, imitators especially in holiness. The apostle concluded his instruction in that previous section by framing that life of sanctification in terms of thankfulness to God: "Giving thanks always for all things unto God and the Father in the name of our Lord Jesus Christ" (v. 20). But the sentence does not stop there. He wants us clearly to understand how that thanks to God is to be expressed. So we read this: "Submitting yourselves one to another in the fear of God" (v. 21). To submit yourselves one to another is to mark your lives as Christians. For those who are given the relationship of marriage, it is also to mark their lives within that relationship. It is not just the wives, therefore, who are to submit to their husbands. We are to submit one to another in the fear of God.

That is what Paul also speaks about in Philippians 2. To be concerned with myself, my name, my advancement, my desires, is the opposite of the calling God gives us as those redeemed by Christ, objects of his love and sacrificial service. Rather, looking not on my own things, I seek the well-being of my spouse, my family, my brothers and sisters in Christ.

It is impossible to have a joyful marriage relationship, just as it is impossible that the church reflects the joy that God would have us experience as his people, if we live with a self-absorbed focus. For a husband to live as if the home revolves around him, or for a wife to manipulate her husband to get her own desires, is to ruin a relationship with the self-centeredness that would cast Christ off his throne.

We must stop making excuses for selfishness and bow in repentance before the cross of him who sought our welfare by living selflessly. He gave himself for our sakes. He sought our interest, even though it cost him his own life. A Christian marriage is the marriage of one man and one woman who as disciples of our Lord Jesus, as those who are partakers of his life, are—for that reason—resolved to deny self and to serve one another. You either selfishly insist on your own way and walk in the opposite direction of your Savior, or you serve one another with joy. And do not forget, our natures are given to the idolatry of self.

The Necessary Mindset

To deny self and to live in the joy of our relationships requires a specific mindset. We are to be Christlike in our dealings with our spouses and with each other.

"Let this mind be in you, which was also in Christ Jesus" (v. 5). And what is that mind? It is his mind as revealed in his willingness to be a servant and to walk in humble obedience to God also in seeking the good of those to whom he stood in a covenantal relationship established by God himself.

The apostle links the mind of Christ, a servant heart, to the very gospel itself.

Think of this in terms of the bride of Christ. We think of marriage in terms of a man and woman building a relationship, the man asking her to marry him, she saying yes, and their marriage taking place. We do not live in a day of a dowry being paid to the father of the bride. For a man to marry in our culture is quite easy. It was not easy for Christ. For the Bridegroom of the church to take to himself that bride, he had to pay a price. Why? Because she was so flawed and had so many faults, was so ugly with sin, that she had fallen under condemnation. She would be cast off, given no place in the fellowship of God and no opportunity to serve him. Those were the consequences she must bear. Her situation was hopeless. But because of the election of grace Christ had his eyes upon her and would not leave her in that wretched state. For all her faults, for all her sins, he would pay the price. He would even die for her, that she might be reconciled unto God. And once she was washed, Christ himself would take her as his own bride. He would cherish her and nourish her and do whatever it took to shape her into what *he* would have her be.

This is the wonder of grace. Have you been a partaker of that wonder? Then whatever thoughts of achievement might be presented by the idolatry of self are seen as only an illusion. We repent of our self-centeredness and fix our eyes upon our bridegroom, Jesus Christ. With his Holy Spirit continually replenishing our lives by the means of grace, we hear his word: "Let this mind be in you, which was also in Christ Jesus."

This is how God would have us live in marriage, in family life, and among his people. Know who you are in your Lord Jesus. Live in the consciousness of what he has done for you.

When we lay hold of the gospel, we are brought low and lifted up—both. That gospel humbles us to see our own ugliness. It also gives us to see the joy of being delivered from our own ugliness. The joy comes from seeing how Christ expended himself for our sakes, to make us beautiful in a way that not only seemed our achievement, but was.

So ought we to love one another, in the home as well as in the church family.

Chapter 14

FORGIVING
ONE ANOTHER

31. Let all bitterness, and wrath, and anger, and clamour, and
    evil speaking, be put away from you, with all malice:
32. And be ye kind one to another, tenderhearted, forgiving
    one another, even as God for Christ's sake hath forgiven
    you.—Ephesians 4:31–32

We have seen in previous chapters that when it comes to a
healthy devotion to living joyfully in marriage, there needs
to be the godly exercise of love, even as Christ also loved the church
and gave himself for her. Therefore, there must be the desire to bring
out the best in each other.

Thus it follows that dying to self is also essential to living joyfully in marriage. The sinfulness of our natures, evident already in
infancy, is that we make idols of self. When we worship ourselves,
there is no room for love and the sacrifices that must be made in
the expression of love. So, in the way of repentance, we are led
once again to Christ and given to see the mind that governed all his
actions toward his heavenly Father and toward us. And we hear the
gospel call in Philippians 2:5, "Let this mind be in you, which was
also in Christ Jesus."

The third essential element to living Christlike in marriage and therefore being dedicated to expressing the joy of the relationship between Christ and his bride is that we understand the importance of forgiving one another. We find that in Ephesians 4:31–32, as well as in many other passages in holy Scripture.

Once again we see that these elements of living joyfully in marriage apply without exception to our relationships within the church, Christ's bride. Repeatedly Scripture points to the requirement of forgiving those who have sinned against us. It sets forth that requirement while at the same time considering the various aspects of forgiveness and of what compels forgiveness.

Forgiveness can only flow from the life of Christ in us, which life has made us very conscious of the wonder of our being forgiven by God, not for anything we have done, but for the perfect work of Jesus Christ on our behalf. This work of Christ is an amazing expression of the riches of the grace of God, as we read in Ephesians 1:7. In Acts 13:38 Paul even speaks of the focus of the preaching being the forgiveness of sins. The preaching therefore works that knowledge of salvation that alone results in a life of thankfulness and a walk of godliness. Where there is not the consciousness of the wonder of having been forgiven, neither will there be a walk that shows the life of that gospel. But you who hear that good news proclaimed, and who have confessed being a partaker of the wonder of forgiveness by the precious blood of Jesus, are called to live in the light of the importance of that gospel, also forgiving one another. We consider that truth especially with application to marriage, while remembering that the calling is the same in our relationships as members of Christ's bride.

Why Forgiveness Is Important

Why is forgiveness an important element in living joyfully in marriage? Because we live as sinners among fellow sinners. Redeemed sinners we are, when by faith we belong to our Savior Jesus Christ;

but sinners still. That is never to be an excuse. That is always to compel us to repentance before God and before one another. But that is the reality for us so long as we live on this earth and in this flesh. We cannot hide from that fact. We are fools to attempt to deny it and to deceive ourselves. We must face it. We must face that sinfulness of our own natures constantly.

It is that stark reality that our Reformed fathers faced when they adopted for use in the Reformed churches the Form for the Confirmation of Marriage before the Church. That form begins this way: "Whereas married persons are generally, by reason of sin, subject to many troubles and afflictions."[1] That is stated not only that we might immediately be humbled before the high, even impossible calling of holy marriage, but that we might be directed to the word of God to see the only possibility for healthy, joyful, God-glorifying marriages, namely, that we live in marriage walking hand-in-hand with God our Father in Jesus Christ.

That statement, the profound and humbling reality that confronts us immediately in the Form for the Confirmation of Marriage, reminds us of two things. First, we live with the effects of sin throughout our lives in this world, always reminded of the temporary nature of our earthly marriages because of death. Second, we also live in these relationships very much affected by the sinfulness of our own natures.

Our young people do well to realize, even though it will not really strike them until they are married, that marriage does not bring you into conflict with that person who is your spouse as much as it brings you into conflict with yourself. Marriage exposes you for what you really are.

In our youth, partially because of our inexperience in life and largely because of our lack of spiritual maturity, we do not really

---

1 Form for the Confirmation of Marriage, in *Confessions and Church Order*, 306.

grasp how sinful we are. Yes, we know that we are sinners. We have had to face the discipline of father and mother from before we can remember. If our parents have been faithful to God's word in their discipline of us, they have not just punished us for our wrongdoings, but they have taken us before God's word to expose the sins of our hearts from which flow those evil doings and to lead us to godly repentance. But the consciousness of the sinfulness of sin is something that develops with spiritual growth and becomes more acute the older we get. And marriage soon exposes how sinful you are.

You begin that life with the person you have confessed to love more than any other human being. But before you know it, you have said something in such a way that it brings conflict into your relationship. The intimacy of marriage, living together in such a close relationship, has the effect of shaking you and forcing you to pay attention to the sinfulness of your own nature. Yes, you can live in denial. Many do. You can refuse to face and to repent of the sin that would rob you of all joy and devastate your relationship—with God and with each other. Many do. But live in denial, and those very sins will enslave you and destroy you. We not only have to face the reality of our own depravity, but we who are married must live with a sinful spouse, even as in the church we who are members of Christ's bride have to live with fellow sinners.

Christianity would be so easy if only it were a matter of Jesus and me. So it seems. But Christianity is Jesus and his bride, a bride with many members. Christianity is a matter of living out of the consciousness of my faith union to Christ *in relationship to* fellow sinners. In fact, God has made the matter of our relationship to others the litmus test of our relationship to him. We read in John 13:35, "By this shall all men know that ye are my disciples, if ye have love one to another." To love one another comes in the realistic setting of having to deal with each other's weaknesses, faults, and sins. We must do that in a way that reveals the love of God toward us, and a dying to self.

We must live in such a way that we assist one another on the way to heaven. That is fundamentally what marriage is all about, a man and a woman given by God to each other, that they might walk together and encourage each other on the difficult pathway to heaven. But let's not forget, that is also true of every relationship established by God within the bride of Christ. Why doesn't God just grab an individual here and an individual there and take them to heaven? Because he would have us realize that we do not stand alone, that we cannot even survive alone, in the waste howling wilderness of this earthly sojourn. We need each other. We need our fellow saints. We need to live in the full communion of the church of Jesus Christ as he establishes it in our given location as a congregation of believers and their children.

Marriage therefore reflects the bigger picture of your life and mine in the bride of Christ. To help each other, to support and strengthen one another, is not only the calling but the desire of every believer who is living in the consciousness of what Christ has done for him or her. At the heart of what Christ has done for us is forgiveness. So are we to forgive one another.

What Forgiveness Involves

There is an inseparable connection between verses 31 and 32 of Ephesians 4.

You will notice from verse 31 that there are several emotions that affect us, and certain actions to which our sinful hearts drive us, when there is a sense of being wronged by someone. We must be conscious of the sinful motivation of malice that stirs all these things within us and actively, with spiritual purpose, put these sins from us. Bitterness, wrath, and anger are specific emotions that arise from a sense of being wronged.

But what is easily forgotten is that these are more than emotions. These are emotional reactions or responses that involve certain perceptions—whether accurate or inaccurate—of certain beliefs and motives, as well as a willing determination either to suppress or—more likely for most—to bring to violent expression those thoughts of our own hearts, whether by words or by actions. The call to repentance that comes to every one of us is the call to put away from ourselves all these sinful responses.

Let's look at each of these very briefly.

Bitterness comes from a term describing a plant that produces poisonous fruit. Think about that. It explains why Hebrews 12:14–15 contrasts the holiness "without which no man shall see the Lord" and the root of bitterness that drives a person from the fellowship of God, not only troubling that bitter person, but defiling many who associate with that person. That is the poisonous fruit of bitterness. Bitterness is an unloving condition that focuses on some perceived deficiency in someone else, never to see any good. Bitterness will turn even imaginary grievances into real ones, and nurse them.

Think of the effects of that in a marriage. In that close relationship, when no faults can be hidden, would you focus on the faults of your spouse? Then bitterness will consume you. Not only that, your bitterness will make life miserable for many around you. You will become a cynical person very few care to be around. Bitterness fuels evil thoughts and poisons the soul. If you choose to focus upon any of life's negatives and things in which you find fault, and refuse to let it go or to address it in a proper biblical way, you will perish in that bitterness of your soul.

Bitterness is a fertilizer to wrath and anger. Generally those two terms are placed in the opposite order. Wrath is the breathing forth of anger. The term *anger* speaks literally of an internal swelling of one's temper, that which might be bottled up within. *Wrath* brings to expression that anger of the heart.

Wrath and anger, it is pointed out, often come to expression in clamor and evil speaking. *Clamor* speaks of an outcry. It can take the form of raised voices, shouting, even shrieking at one another. It can be expressed by crying. It can take the form of reviling, threatening, even mocking, which all cross over into the next concept, that of evil speaking. And *evil speaking*, a sin of which we are all aware, is deliberately saying things that are harmful to others.

All these things flow from the fountain of *malice,* the malice of our own sinful hearts and minds. Malice is the evil source of all this wickedness. Malice is the determination to be hurtful. And what is that but the hatred that is deeply rooted in the depravity of our natures?

Once again in this text we are called to stand before the reality of our own sinfulness. If we have not faced this sinfulness of our own natures in heartfelt repentance before God, it will be impossible for us to carry out the positive calling to forgive one another. Facing personal sin comes before dealing with the sins of others. If we carry bitterness like a treasure to be guarded, we have no heart for forgiveness.

What is demonstrated in Ephesians 4:32, however, is the fact that we cannot live in the joy of the Christian life, and we cannot live in the joy of marriage, except we root out the negative while at the same time nurturing the positive. Martyn Lloyd-Jones, in a sermon on this text, used an illustration to demonstrate this truth. He pointed to the fact that the dead leaves of the trees in wintertime do not have to be plucked off by people. But with some trees in particular, "it is the new life, the shoot that comes and pushes off the dead in order to make room for itself."[2] In a similar way, for us who are partakers of the new life in Christ, we get rid of the sinful expressions of our evil hearts especially by developing the new virtues of Christ's life that is in us. As those new virtues develop and grow, they

---

2   Martyn Lloyd-Jones, *Darkness and Light: An Exposition of Ephesians 4:17–5:17* (Grand Rapids, MI: Baker Book House, 1982), 283.

increasingly push out of our lives the malice and all that flows from that sinful determination of our evil natures.

Once again you see the importance of growing in the life of Christ and the consciousness of who he is for us and in us. From the life of Christ and his sanctifying Spirit comes his word with powerful application, "And be ye kind one to another, tenderhearted, forgiving one another, even as God for Christ's sake hath forgiven you" (Eph. 4:32).

To be kind one to another, tenderhearted, illustrates the fact that forgiving one another follows the two essentials to living joyfully in marriage that we considered previously. Both kindness and tenderheartedness imply the principle of love in your heart. Both also imply that you are no longer self-centered but have an eye to the needs of your spouse or fellow Christian. Kindness is one of the expressions of love. Tenderheartedness is such a focus on the other that you know their distress and are moved to compassion. But these things culminate in the calling to forgive one another. When these are present, there will be a willingness, even a longing, to forgive.

The forgiveness of which the inspired apostle speaks is that which treats a person better than he or she deserves. There are two words in the New Testament that are properly translated "to forgive." The one word expresses the sense of "letting go." But the word used here is much more demanding. It calls us to repair the brokenness by bearing the cost. The one word has to do with damage control to our own souls, letting go so that we are not consumed by bitterness and anger. But this word speaks of rebuilding. And it speaks of rebuilding at *my* cost and *my* effort. Forgive one another.

The question naturally arises: But doesn't that presuppose the *seeking* of forgiveness? Doesn't that require repentance on the part of the one who has wronged me, even my spouse? Let's look at those questions.

First, if by the seeking of forgiveness you are sitting back waiting for your spouse to come to you to confess wrong, the answer is no. According to the meaning of the word used here, *you* are to begin the rebuilding process, even if it requires you to bear the cost. That means, for one thing, there is to be found in you a willingness to forgive, rooted in your love. So profound is the love Christ has shed abroad in our hearts by his Holy Spirit that 1 Peter 4:8 tells us that love shall cover a multitude of sins. That is why we are able to think charitably one toward another. That is why in marriage we do not demand the expression of repentance for every sin observed, because we can see the sorrow of our spouse and are eager to forgive.

But where that sorrow of repentance is not evident, the second question comes into play: "Doesn't forgiveness require repentance on the part of the one who has wronged me?" Yes, it does. That is why our Lord instructs us repeatedly to admonish one another, to go to each other with the desire to lead to repentance. This is necessary to begin the rebuilding process required of us in forgiving each other as we are called to in this text. But we are to confront with a readiness, even a desire to forgive, and that in the full awareness of what God has done in forgiving us.

When we reflect on the last clause of Ephesians 4:31–32, "even as God for Christ's sake hath forgiven you," we must not fail to reflect once again on that work of Christ. That also says something about what this forgiveness involves, especially insofar as the husband in marriage is to represent Christ. If the husband is to represent Christ in his headship, his leadership in the home, the husband must take the lead also in reconciliation. In that relationship between Christ and the church, who took the lead in making things right? It was not the church, was it? Christ himself came from the throne to show his love and mercy at Calvary. Christ is the one who again and again pursues his wayward bride to seek reconciliation. Christ was the one who came to Peter after Peter's denials of him. And in your own relationship to Jesus Christ, who is the one who has come to you again and again to draw you to himself in forgiving love?

So, husbands, belonging to your leadership is also this, that you lead in making things right. There are times, of course, when wives should say, "I have sinned in this way; I am sorry." But if husbands look to their wives to take the lead and sit by in an icy silence waiting for things to be made right, they show themselves failures as leaders. Here too, husbands are to reflect the leadership of Christ in taking the initiative toward bringing about reconciliation.

So how are you to do this? For one thing, when you have seen your own fault before God, you will humble yourself before your wife—and family, if need be—and confess your sin. Bear in mind, that is not just to say, "I know I wasn't right." It is to confess the sin specifically, so that your wife clearly sees that you understand the way in which you sinned. Then go to the word of God together. If you are going to do this, then you have given thought to this. True repentance is not a flippant action. It is a thoughtful action. It is an act that also lays hold of God's word and the promises of God for forgiveness and cleansing when we confess our sins before him.

This brings us back to the need to deny ourselves. A man can be so full of pride that the very thought of confessing sin even to his wife makes him tense up with the desire to protect himself and his pride. Do not let that pride consume you. There can be no joy in the way of impenitence. God gives no peace to those who insist on clinging to the idolatry of self. But when you humble yourself before God and lay bare your sins in heartfelt repentance, not only before God but before that spouse (or brother or sister) whom you have hurt, not only will that oppressive guilt be gone with the sense of failure that accompanies it, but the tensions of your marriage will be replaced by the joy that God would have your marriage express.

What Forgiveness Reveals

The text, in calling us to forgive one another, "even as God for Christ's sake hath forgiven you," reminds us that forgiveness is inseparable from the grace of God by which alone we are saved. To forgive one another is to lift our marriages out of a perspective that can only repeatedly fuel disappointment, bitterness, and anger into the clear light of God's glorious grace. It is to keep the focus of our marriages, and our relationships in the church, upon Christ.

The Bible expresses the profound reality of this truth and its importance by describing us and our sin in terms of committing adultery. By our sins—and sins committed repeatedly, mind you—we have so offended God, so severed our relationship to Christ, that the Bible terms us "adulterers and adulteresses."

That Christ has established such a relationship with us that it is termed "marriage," and defined in Scripture as *unbreakable*, indicates the magnitude of God's grace toward us in Christ Jesus. Our marriage to him is established entirely upon the basis of grace, grace revealed in the sacrifice of himself upon the cross that he might take us to himself and reconcile us unto God. Our marriage to Christ is maintained faithfully by him on the basis of his own unchangeable love toward us.

If, by the Spirit's work in our hearts through the gospel, we live in the consciousness of that amazing wonder of God's grace revealed to us and bestowed upon us in Christ Jesus our Lord, then our marriages and our lives will reflect that. Only then will our marriages and our lives reveal that grace as expressed in the words of Ephesians 4:31–32. Christ laid down his life for us to make us his beautiful bride. He reached out to draw us to himself and to reconcile us unto God. He led us to repentance, gave us faith, and bestows his love upon us in such a way that, even when we fail him, we know that he will not forsake us. So great is his love toward us!

The joy of living in the light of that truth gives you the desire to give the same love to your spouse and to one another for Christ's sake. So we can say to each other, "I see your sin, my love; but I can cover it with forgiveness, because Jesus saw my sin and covered it." We see in each other the beauty of the grace of God, and rejoice.

Chapter 15

PULLING THE WEEDS OUT OF OUR GARDENS[1]

30. I went by the field of the slothful, and by the vineyard of the man void of understanding;

31. And, lo, it was all grown over with thorns, and nettles had covered the face thereof, and the stone wall thereof was broken down.—Proverbs 24:30–31

The words of Proverbs 24:30–31 paint a sorry picture of "the man void of understanding." It is quite the contrast to our theme of living joyfully in marriage. When we consider joyful marriage as the result of much effort, even intensity of labor by the husband or wife who is one by faith in Christ Jesus and who therefore bears the fruit of faith, then "the man void of understanding" is not an example of one who will be living joyfully in marriage.

But in this text there is also another figure we do well to consider: a vineyard or garden full of weeds. We know how quickly weeds grow and how they thrive in an unattended garden. They soon choke out all the desirable fruit that a well-tended garden will bear.

---

1   The idea of this chapter was derived from chapter 7, "Pulling Weeds," in Paul David Tripp's *What Did You Expect? Redeeming the Realities of Marriage* (Wheaton, IL: Crossway, 2010), 101–14.

We have seen that an essential to our devotion to expressing the joy in marriage is forgiving one another. Forgiveness involves not only rooting out the negative, addressing what is wrong, but nurturing the positive as well. To forgive one another is to lift our marriages out of a perspective that can only repeatedly fuel disappointment, bitterness, and anger into the clear light of God's glorious grace. It is to keep the focus of our marriages, as well as our relationships in the church, upon Christ and the magnitude of his grace toward us.

To forgive one another belongs to the essential *labors* to which God calls us in our relationships in the church and in the intimate relationship that is marriage. But underlying the concept of forgiveness is the humble labor of pulling the weeds out of our own gardens. Solomon speaks this proverb to set forth a spiritual reality.

A Powerful Figure

The figure Solomon sets before us in Proverbs 24:30–31 is powerful and readily understood. The figure is that of a small farm of a Hebrew householder. That little farm had two dominant features, its vineyard and its stone wall. At one time it had been the place of a man's dreams, built by hard work. Whether by inheritance or by purchase, a man had obtained this piece of ground in the hilly terrain of Judah.

The *field* referred to in the text was an open piece of land, cleared of its trees. Perhaps the original householder had even put his own shoulders to the clearing of that land of his dreams. He had something in mind for that land, something beautiful. On that cleared land he had gone to work, cultivating the ground, moving rocks, tilling the soil, and planting a vineyard on a sunny slope. Although the text does not speak of his house, we may suppose that he also built a house there—what we would probably call a cottage, a humble abode where he and his wife could raise their family. He also put a great deal of work into building a stone wall. He did not have any heavy equipment to do that work. Everything had to be done by hand. But he took the large stones from his fields and laid out and built a beautiful stone wall.

The text does not say anything about the original householder, other than to show that the original work had been one of clear devotion and hard work—similar to that of any joyful marriage and home. Whenever you observe a man and woman happily married, whose home life is clearly blessed by God, you may understand that the blessing has been the fruit of clear devotion and hard work, established upon the foundation of Christ, through faith in him, and according to his word.

But in course of time, the man who presently owned that farm became the object of Solomon's study as Solomon passed by that property in his kingdom. The original owner of the property had likely gone the way of all flesh. We do not know if this was one of his sons who had taken over the property, or someone farther removed in time. But the present owner of this land did not have the dream for the property that the original owner had. He did not have the same interest in the property.

You know, if not by experience then certainly by observation, that the upkeep of property is no little task. If you picture this property with its vineyard, a garden, and its stone walls, you realize that it takes a lot of work to maintain such a property. Not many people are interested in that kind of work. Stone walls are beautiful, until time and the effects of rain and the freeze-thaw cycle start to eat away the mortar. The mortar back then, being mostly mud, did not have the strength of the mortar today.

In addition, once the land is tilled and cultivated, a vineyard will produce more weeds and thistles, if left to itself, than would unclaimed and unworked land. Vines run rampant when left unpruned. Solomon looked at this scene, where once had been a well-kept and fruitful piece of property, the joy of its owner, "and, lo, it was all grown over with thorns, and nettles had covered the face thereof, and the stone wall thereof was broken down" (v. 31). It was a mess.

The explanation is given us by the wise preacher. The field was now owned by a slothful or lazy man. The vineyard now manifested that its owner was one void of understanding. That is a powerful and sad description of a person—slothful or lazy and void of understanding.

I want you to note well, the man whose property Solomon evaluated was not a criminal. He did not steal from people. He did not rely on other people's support. The text does not present a man who wasted his time involving himself in other men's matters. He might have been known—to use language of our modern time—as a fine Christian man, just a little sloppy. But Solomon examines his estate and, according to the evidence, judges the man lazy.

The lazy man plods along, not really devoted to the calling God has given him. He might convince himself that what he has done is "good enough." He might think, "My marriage, my family life, is good enough." He might use the excuse that he does not like to do this or that but has done what is necessary for him to do. But he stands before the calling God has given him and does not do it.

Furthermore, Solomon refers to him as "a man void of understanding." That might seem a rather harsh, even incorrect, judgment. After all, the man owned a vineyard, a house, and property. He certainly had some intellectual capability. Yet Solomon speaks of him as "a man void of understanding." The word Solomon uses in that connection refers to the source of understanding. That means this man did not have the spiritual heart necessary for a proper understanding of God, of our relationship to him, and of our calling in this world as we live before God's face. He showed himself unconverted.

"Now wait a minute," you might object. "This man was a child of Judah! He was a citizen of Solomon's kingdom. He certainly knew

Jehovah! He certainly knew the testimony of God's word, at least to some degree."

What you say is undoubtedly the case. That makes Solomon's judgment all the more serious. What this demonstrates, you see, is a truth found throughout Scripture. It is, in fact, a truth found with emphasis throughout the Bible. True understanding is a spiritual virtue, belonging only to the one who stands united to Christ by the living bond of faith.

What Solomon says here is helpful from a practical point of view in understanding the actions not only of unbelievers, but even in the church world. Many people in the course of time, and in the church even today, bring to expression from many different perspectives what Solomon observed in this text.

I think of a businessman I once knew, a confessing Christian, who was known in the business community and among his employees as cutthroat, unethical, do whatever it takes to make money. When confronted with the fact that his behavior as a businessman was not in harmony with his confession as a Christian, his response was, "My Christian faith is for Sunday; it has nothing to do with my business!" He was a man void of understanding, whose knowledge of Scripture was only useful, and that in the most general way, on Sunday. When it came to his calling to apply the word preached to his daily life, including how he operated his business and treated his employees, he was spiritually lazy, something that Solomon demonstrates is indicative of an empty-headed religion. He had no true spiritual understanding, because he knew not Christ who is Lord of our lives in every respect.

There have been those in the church, in Reformed churches, who could accurately set forth many biblical teachings of the Reformed faith—teachings such as the absolute sovereignty of God, unconditional election, the definite atonement and sovereignly wrought salvation of the elect alone—but whose lives were not governed by those beautiful truths of Scripture. I have ministered to those who, whenever the commandments or precepts of God's word were pressed upon them, acted as if they were addressed to everyone but themselves. They were above having their own lives called into question by the penetrating word of God. They chafed whenever they heard the words "responsibility" or "accountability" and strenuously resisted the call to sanctification. Some would refer to them as practical antinomians. The problem is much deeper. They are unbelievers. They don't know what it is to be married to Christ, to be one with him by a true and living faith.

Solomon's judgment is helpful in understanding where such people are coming from. They are void of understanding. They might consider themselves to be standards of orthodoxy. They would quickly judge those who do not agree with them. They are quick to blame others, even their spouses, but refuse to confess their own sins. "Void of understanding." Their spiritual laziness is indicative of their lack of spiritual life and therefore their lack of spiritual understanding. Otherwise they would be humbled by the wonder that God has predestinated us and saved us in Christ, has given us life in his Son, that we might show forth his praise.

We are indeed his workmanship, as we read in Ephesians 2:10. But "we are his workmanship," as that text says, "created in Christ Jesus unto good works, which God hath before ordained that we should walk in them." When we who are in Christ Jesus see the wonder work of God's grace in us, we humbly confess our specific sins and our sinfulness, acknowledge the wonder of his grace in saving us, and realize that our salvation came from nothing in us. But we also acknowledge even daily the wonder, as we read in Philippians 2:13, that "it is God which worketh in you both to will and to do of his good pleasure," and therefore he works in such a way that we enter into that work, laboring in the calling he has given us to "work out your own salvation with fear and trembling" (v. 12).

To sit back and be a lazy Christian, to fail to apply what we hear in the gospel, is to serve as an illustration of what Solomon observed and wrote about in Proverbs 24:30–31.

Others show themselves zealous when it comes to the work of the church. They will readily involve themselves in everything. But they will do so to the neglect of the garden that is their own home life. I have known men who appeared so pious among their fellow church members, but whose homes were in shambles. They were abusive to their children. They were rarely there for their wives. They failed to nurture their family in the love of Christ with spiritual instruction and godliness. They were strangers to working in their *own* gardens. In time their estates were seen as those described here by Solomon, overgrown with worldliness, children defining Christianity by their absentee fathers and running the other way. Such men illustrated why Paul had to instruct Timothy concerning officebearers that if a man know not how to rule his own house, how shall he take care of the church of God?

How, then, do we live? Do we live as those who belong to Jesus Christ, those who have been redeemed by the sovereign wonder of God's grace at great price, even the precious blood of his own dear Son? Do we recognize the treasure that God has given us—as did the original householder of that property—so that we devote ourselves to putting that treasure to use and seeing it bring forth the most beautiful fruits? Do we show ourselves those who have spiritual understanding that comes from being one with Christ?

A Pointed Application

Here is an application for the entire Christian life.

There is an element in this text that must not be overlooked. It is an element that has us face the reality of sin. That, after all, is the origin of those thorns and nettles that had overgrown this property Solomon observed. Because the creation speaks of death and the outpouring of God's wrath, we always must go to the Scripture to understand the higher things of God revealed to us in the creation. But the creation does speak. And in the light of God's word, the creation speaks so profoundly that we could spend a lifetime studying it and not even scratch the surface. Children go to school that they might learn the foundational principles in studying the things of God's creation. But learn those principles, learn to look at this marvelous creation in the light of God's word, and you will not have to pay tuition to advance your education. Just look around you with attentive eyes and give thought to what you see in the light of the Scriptures.

Solomon saw that weeds grow without effort. It belongs to the natural order of things since the fall. The same is true in our own lives when it comes to sin. It is one thing to water our gardens. That is necessary. But if you do not weed that garden, watering will only fuel the growth of the weeds until they choke out any fruitful plants in that garden.

There are many Christians in name who, like the Pharisees, are zealous in focusing on the trivial as well as on rules, some of which may be not so trivial but important. If we are not dealing with the issues of our own hearts, if we are not facing the weeds in our own gardens, if we are not laboring to root out those sins, then we shall bear the evil fruits of our spiritual laziness, the thorns and thistles and broken-down walls. Our hopes and our dreams, especially for the generations that follow us, will be shattered.

One thing we have seen repeatedly—not just in this book on marriage, but as a theme that runs throughout the gospel. We are not going to deal with sin in a proper way, we are not going to be weeding our gardens, unless Jesus Christ and his work and our relationship to him is on the foreground of our thinking. The Bridegroom must be the object of our love, to do his will the object of our desire. Otherwise our religion is empty.

There is a theme that underlies the instruction of this text. It is the theme that lies at the heart of all the Proverbs, being explicitly set forth in many chapters of this book, including chapter 24. We find it in the opening words of verse 21, "My son, fear thou the LORD [Jehovah]." To fear the Lord is to live in such love for him, with such devotion to his cause, that you are afraid to do anything that would offend him. To live in such love for him is to see him not only as your heavenly Father, but as your Savior, who loved you from eternity. It is to see him in the face of Jesus Christ, your bridegroom. Only by gazing upon him with that sense of awe and love will you delight to do his will.

The Christian life, after all, is not a life of serving God with drudgery, as if such servitude is beyond one as important as *I*. The Christian life is serving God. Yes, that is hard work. But it is a service of love. It comes from the sense of the privilege that I may live in such a relationship with the living God, redeemed by Christ.

But the application of the text is pointed especially for Christian marriage. The application is not something I make haphazardly. It is an application with biblical grounds, found in the inspired writings of this same Solomon. For in the Song of Solomon, where the relationship of marriage is unfolded in its most glorious application as the relationship of Christ to his bride the church, Solomon repeatedly refers to that marriage in terms of a garden, a fruitful garden of many beautiful plants. We read in the fourth chapter of the Song of Solomon:

12. A garden inclosed is my sister, my spouse; a spring shut up, a fountain sealed.
13. Thy plants are an orchard of pomegranates, with pleasant fruits; camphire, with spikenard,
14. Spikenard and saffron; calamus and cinnamon, with all trees of frankincense; myrrh and aloes, with all the chief spices:

15. A fountain of gardens, a well of living waters, and streams from Lebanon.

16. Awake, O north wind; and come, thou south; blow upon my garden, that the spices thereof may flow out. Let my beloved come into his garden, and eat his pleasant fruits. (Song of Sol. 4:12–16)

The following chapter opens with the words, "I have come into my garden, my sister, my spouse."

Solomon himself knew the application that I make here and very likely reflected personally with no little sorrow as he spoke this proverb to his son. The application is as plain to marriage as to any other aspect of the Christian life; perhaps more so.

Those who receive from God the gift of marriage always enter that relationship with the same dreams as the original householder of the estate that Solomon observed. But we begin married life not as some fairy tale. The dreams and hopes we have at the beginning of that relationship must be looked at in the same way the original householder looked at that land when it was still barren. He saw potential. But he knew that if he was going to see the fulfillment of that potential, he would have to commit himself to a lasting, even lifelong labor. It must be a labor of love.

A fruitful garden begins with hard work. Clearing the land is hard work. So is preparing for a lasting relationship. Clearing that land involves, as we have seen, taking the ax to the tree of self and bringing that idol down. Clearing the land is only the first step. The land must be cultivated too. It does not cultivate itself. Young adults are not automatically prepared for marriage. They must cultivate their spiritual lives in order to prepare for marriage, if marriage may be God's will for them.

But the work does not end once the garden is planted. That work continues.

Pulling the Weeds Out of Our Gardens

At first it can even be rather tedious. There are many adjustments to be made in establishing a home where two have become one. Those adjustments are all the more difficult because of inexperience. This kind of work involved in marriage is new. The husband must adjust to his new role as the spiritual head of the home. That is work to which he is unaccustomed. It is a new line of work, as it were. The same is true for the young woman, who must learn just what it is to be a wife, a homemaker. Even though mother taught her many things about certain aspects of being a wife, the difference is as great as reading an instruction manual and actually doing something. She has to adjust to her new labors as a wife.

The couple also must work at developing their relationship, learning to work as a team. Just as one does not become a master gardener without many years of experience, so it is in the home. There is never a time when we can be lazy in a marriage relationship and expect it to be healthy.

Moreover, as the text reminds us and as we know only too well from experience, the garden does not grow without weeds manifesting themselves. Those weeds are the sins that would readily choke out the fruitfulness and joy of married life.

Solomon looks at this scene and would have us realize that we are not going to have our marriages and relationships in the church thrive if we are not committed to pulling the weeds out of our gardens. We talked about clearing the land by taking the ax to the root of the tree that is self-centeredness. But that chopped-down tree is of such a variety that it quickly sends out new shoots. The weeds, the choking growth, would reestablish themselves. To the degree that we let the weeds grow, they will begin to affect for ill our relationship.

Solomon could tell us from experience how miserable married life is when it is not planted well and when it is not cared for properly. The text before us shows the fruits, *evil* fruits, of neglect also in married life. That neglect often comes to expression just in our inattentiveness to one another. How can you nurture your garden when you pay no attention or little attention to it? The work for this vineyard and garden requires commitment.

Furthermore, when two become one, the tending to the garden of that covenantal home becomes the commitment of both. That means there must be communication, so that there is united commitment, teamwork, given to the nurturing of the garden.

Marriage is not a game, with a trophy for one. It is not battling for a position. It is a united commitment to the nurturing of the garden. It is a united commitment to pulling out the weeds that stifle the joyful fruits that are to be expected in a marriage established by Christ. The work required of us—and yes, it is required—is that we confront the weeds in our personal lives, the sins as well as the weaknesses, knowing that if we let them go, they will ultimately choke out every last bit of joy and happiness.

But let's not forget, whether we talk about marriage or our life in the various relationships God gives us within his bride the church, we are called to reflect the mystery, the marriage of Christ and his bride. What our religion amounts to will be seen in exactly this, our faithfulness to the calling God gives us and the labors he entrusts to us, beginning in the home. Solomon would learn through painful experience the necessity of living close to Jehovah, in the consciousness of the Messiah, Jesus Christ.

It is easy to make excuses when it comes to our neglect of the garden. The slothful man, void of understanding, can speak of his need for sleep and his good intentions of getting to the work soon. But when we understand our dependence upon our Lord Jesus Christ and the work of his Holy Spirit to overcome the weeds that so quickly arise in our own sinful natures, then we will find our strength in his word.

Have you been faithful in pulling out the weeds in the garden of your marriage, the weeds that affect your relationships within the church? God, having created us in Christ Jesus unto good works, points us to the garden and to the work required of us and says, "Get to work, walk in obedience to my word, and you shall see fruits in abundance."

Chapter 16

CAREFUL
COMMUNICATION

Let no corrupt communication proceed out of your mouth, but that which is good to the use of edifying, that it may minister grace unto the hearers.—Ephesians 4:29

The importance of careful communication cannot be emphasized too strongly. We learn already from the creation account in Genesis that God created man after his own image and in his own likeness. Belonging to that is the fact that man was created to communicate. He was given ears to listen and a mouth to speak, with a mind to process both what he hears and what he says. Man was so created, both male and female, that they might have fellowship with God and with one another. They were created that way in order to be able to experience and enjoy fellowship with God, who himself is the communicative God.

Communication is the expression of the covenantal fellowship and love that exists within God himself as three distinct persons in one divine being. For that reason communication is also the expression of our own enjoyment in the fellowship of God's covenantal life. If we are to reflect that life with its joy, there must be careful communication. That is evident from Ephesians 4:29.

Putting Away the Rottenness

When I speak of careful communication in terms of putting away the rottenness, I am calling attention to the opening words of the text: "Let no corrupt communication proceed out of your mouth."

When speaking of *corrupt* communication, Paul uses a term that describes that which is rotten. It is corrupt in the same way that a decaying animal corpse is corrupt. It is not edible. It is useful for nothing. It only throws off a rotting stench and continues its decay.

We must remember that communication is the expression of what is in the heart. It is evident also from what follows in the text that Paul is not speaking merely of avoiding certain words or of being hesitant in what we say. Those things are necessary. The book of Proverbs in many places speaks of the foolishness of hasty speech. Proverbs 10:19 is one example: "In the multitude of words there wanteth not sin: but he that refraineth his lips is wise." But the apostle in Ephesians 4:29 wants us to face the *purpose* of our speech, that which motivates what we say.

How we communicate is a heart issue. What we say is an expression of the heart. That is what our Lord tells us in Luke 6:45: "A good man out of the good treasure of his heart bringeth forth that which is good; and an evil man out of the evil treasure of his heart bringeth forth that which is evil: for of the abundance of the heart his mouth speaketh." He expands upon that in Matthew 12:36–37, with these words of warning: "But I say unto you, That every idle word that men shall speak, they shall give account thereof in the day of judgment. For by thy words thou shalt be justified, and by thy words thou shalt be condemned."

We can so quickly speak without thinking. Do we think that in marriage we can just immediately blurt out whatever is on our mind? "By thy words thou shalt be justified, and by thy words thou shalt be condemned." That is true because those words reveal what is in our hearts. It is important to understand this, in order that we might face the heart issues that affect our communication or lack thereof. Putting away the rottenness addresses the failure to communicate as well as speaking in a way that is not right spiritually.

For various reasons some people do not communicate well.

There are those, for example, who have had very troubled relationships growing up, those whose home life, perhaps, has been very chaotic, with father and mother fighting or siblings causing all kinds of trouble, those who even have suffered father and mother divorcing, who as a result bottle up all kinds of emotional baggage as a way of self-protection. They have been hurt so often, just by what has happened in the home, that they have very little trust in anyone and therefore are afraid to open up even to those close to them.

Others do not communicate well because when they have been open, they have been burned. Someone has betrayed their trust; so they isolate themselves and do not open up to anyone. There are issues of the heart that must be dealt with in a biblical way. A new spiritual perspective must be taken, in order for that person to be able to learn to communicate in a godly way.

Some do not communicate well because they are too absorbed with self-interests. Communication has a theological foundation. God created us with the ability to communicate that we might live in fellowship, being partakers of his covenantal life. We were created to live, not individualistically, but in community. That community might take the form of marriage, or it might take the form of fellowship in the body of Christ, the church, seeing marriage as a reflection of the marriage between Christ and the church. But we were created to live in fellowship. Those who break that community to serve their own self-interests violate the very purpose for which God created us.

Even when we speak of the need for a personal relationship with our heavenly Father through faith in Jesus Christ, we speak of the union that comes to expression in fellowship with God and his people. When we baptize our children, laying hold of the promise of

God to Abraham in Genesis 17:7, we must remember that God established his covenant not just with Abraham as an individual, but with Abraham's spiritual seed, with a people in Christ Jesus.

When we talk about communication therefore, we must realize that one of Satan's chief projects in his attempt to destroy the church has been his effort to bring about the demise of healthy communication and fellowship, particularly in marriage and family life.

I am old enough vaguely to remember the early years of television, when televisions were still so expensive that they were found in very few homes. Before television, when you walked into the main living area of the home, usually called the living room, you would see the furniture arranged in a circle around the room, because that is where the family gathered together for fellowship. That fellowship did not always involve conversation. Sometimes the family would sit and read or play games. But in some homes that fellowship involved conversations about the day, about the issues of the day, about religion and politics. In some homes that fellowship included family devotions or singing, beyond that which may have been conducted at the dinner table. Often the conversations in those living rooms included visitors in the home, neighbors or extended family members who stopped by or people who were invited over for fellowship.

Now we can observe how television has affected family life and particularly communication in the home. In many homes today the living room has been replaced by a room called the family room. When you examine that family room, you will find that the furniture has been arranged to face the wall where is mounted the television. And in many homes today, that television is on from the time the children get home from school and the parents are home from work until the last family member goes to bed at night. What do you think that has done to family fellowship, to communication in the home?

Years ago ministers addressed the issue of drama, and particularly going to the movies, as being contrary to the Christian life of the antithesis. Today the issue is not going to the movies. The movies are in the homes. It is possible, and even important, to consider the content of such dramatic productions, even from the viewpoint of the manifest ungodliness of taking pleasure in those who bring to expression the very sins that make them worthy of everlasting damnation (Rom. 1:32). The content of almost all television programming today makes it off limits to the spiritually minded child of God.

But here we have another issue, and what I consider the most significant issue. Even before Satan was able to have his way with the most defiled content that television programming portrays today, back when the content was much more tame, so to speak, Satan saw the damage he could do by destroying family fellowship and communication.

Now add to that the computer and our smartphones and all the other devices of entertainment. Useful tools these all can be. But they are also instruments in the devil's hands to consume us in our self-centeredness and to lay waste the communication that is the very means for fellowship with God and with one another.

I recently read a report about cell phone addiction among college students, which stated that women reported spending 600 minutes a day on their cell phones, with men somewhat less at 459 minutes a day.[1] People are not talking on the phone for that amount of time. That cell phone use includes internet surfing, more than an hour and a half each day texting, the use of social media, online gaming (a big thing), perhaps watching movies or sporting events and the like. Ten hours a day! Seventy hours a week! Think of that in terms of a forty-hour work week. That is like devoting the time of two full-time jobs to playing on your phone! Cyber addiction has become

---

1 James A. Roberts, Luc Honore Petnji Yaya, and Chris Manolis, "The invisible addiction: Cellphone activities and addiction among male and female college students," *Journal of Behavioral Addictions*, August 26, 2014, accessed September 4, 2020, https://akademiai.com/doi/pdf/10.1556/JBA.3.2014.015.

such a problem that there are organizations and treatment centers to treat those who are addicted to smartphones, social media, and the internet, including internet gaming and gambling.

Don't think Satan doesn't know what he is doing!

What kind of fellowship is found between husband and wife when during the relatively brief time they spend together during the day—perhaps a little bit in the morning, and but a few hours from the time the husband gets home from work until they go to bed—they are each on his or her phone, perhaps one playing games and the other on Facebook, or one on the internet and the other watching television?

If the fellowship of covenantal life comes to expression in conversation, then how does your marriage reflect the relationship of Christ and the church? Communication does not take place when your mind is focused on your phone screen or that computer monitor, and when you simply respond with stony gaze, "uh-huh, yes," when your wife or your husband is trying to say something to you.

God intended communication to take place by listening and speaking.

That means, first, taking the time for fellowship together and making sure that nothing robs us of that time for conversation. All the more important that is when you have children, because they will take much of your time and attention in those evening hours. A husband and wife must have time for conversation together. If that means hiring a babysitter at regular intervals or leaving the children with family members or friends and taking their children another time to give them the same opportunity, it is important that there be time given to effective conversation and communication between husband and wife. There is a rottenness in that relationship where there is no healthy conversation.

There is also a rottenness where communication has been stifled by other sin issues of the heart. That is why the apostle would have us immediately put away from ourselves those sins that grieve the Holy Spirit—bitterness and wrath and anger and clamor and evil speaking, with all malice. We go back to the instruction we received previously on the importance of weeding our own gardens, as well as forgiving one another.

Besides seeing to it that we have time for communication, we also must be sure that our speech fits the Christian life. Is it speech that reflects Christ's life in us? We constantly have to confront the sin issues of our hearts; but we must also realize that the Christian life is one of a constant battle against the sins of our natures. Even when we desire our speech always to be God-glorifying, there are times when the sinfulness of our natures comes to expression in what we say or how we speak.

The apostle in the context is telling us to remember who we are. You are one whom God has saved! You are one who must continually grow as a member of Christ by faith. You have been given the new man, having heard Christ and having been taught by him. For that reason, let no corrupt communication proceed out of your mouth.

Whereas the life of the unregenerate person reflects his idolatry of self, and his speech is an expression of his self-interests and an opportunity to display his own opinions, let it not be so in you. Do not let your speech in your home reflect the arrogance of the ungodly, the selfishness, the excess and lack of discernment. Do not blurt whatever comes to mind. What hurt we can cause with our tongues! We do well to read James 3 regularly and to pray for grace to guard our tongues.

How many relationships are destroyed by criticism? Think about it. If what you regularly hear from your spouse are cutting words, words reflective of a critical spirit that is always looking for failure, for something wrong, how do you respond to that? I dare say your response will be one of withdrawal. Who cares to have fellowship with one whose words express the rottenness of his or her soul?

Rotten food does not nourish but sickens. Rotten food smells bad too and makes people want to leave the room as quickly as possible. So it is with rottenness of speech.

Think about how you speak to your spouse, to your children. Think about how you speak about fellow church members. "Let no corrupt communication proceed out of your mouth."

Some have a gift of speaking. They can easily enter into conversation, even guide or carry a conversation if need be. That can be a blessed gift, when used to God's glory. It can be a curse, when left unguarded. Remember what Jesus said, "For by thy words thou shalt be justified, and by thy words thou shalt be condemned" (Matt. 12:37). When there is rottenness in your speech, it is time to deal with the heart sins from which that speech comes and to flee to the cross in the godly sorrow of repentance.

Communicating Purposefully

Careful communication means that we communicate purposefully. The text defines communicating purposefully by two things. First is "that which is good to the use of edifying" (Eph. 4:29).

We must notice from the text that careful communication is defined by that which is helpful to another. Speech is not about self. It is not about getting what I want. It is not an opportunity for self-display. Yes, communication in marriage is important from every perspective. It is important that your spouse knows your needs, your desires, your joys, your sorrows. Your spouse cannot possibly respond to those needs or desires if you do not express them. But we must remember, in light of the ever-present necessity of dying to self, that careful communication is that which focuses not on myself, but on my spouse. If all you do is tell your spouse what you want from him or her, you are not communicating fruitfully.

Communication begins with listening and observing. The book of Proverbs points to listening as the most important element of communication. How well do we listen to each other? That which is "good" to the use of edifying is that which fits the occasion, that which serves the particular necessity for building up our spouse, our child, our fellow church member. If careful communication is to be that which is helpful, that which fits the occasion and serves to strengthen one another, then we need to listen and observe in order to communicate in a proper way. Listening is a gift. But listening also must be learned. We are not to talk and talk and talk. We are to *communicate* as a part of godly fellowship. To do so we must take the time to listen and to learn to understand the needs of our spouse and our fellow church members.

Careful communication therefore requires wisdom and understanding, even patience. It requires also a biblical understanding and perspective that you can apply to the need at hand. Wisdom, after all, is not just common sense, but the ability to apply the word of God to that which we observe and face and the situations in which God places us.

To use an example: Do you see your wife's frustration building after a couple difficult days with the children? Do you ignore that and start talking about yourself and your needs and wants and frustrations? Then you are not really helping her, are you? Don't you think it would be more helpful to tell her, "I can see the children are getting to you; let me take care of them for a couple hours while you relax"? Or "Tomorrow we're going to get so-and-so to babysit, while you and I go out to eat and to talk." Or if the money is tight—as it often is when you have a family—this is the time to drop the kids off at family or friends for a while, giving them the opportunity to do the same another time. And how often do you tell your wife how much you appreciate her and how important she is to you and to your family?

How well do you wives communicate to your husbands? How well do you listen and observe? Do you speak in a way that honors him, that strengthens him, that encourages him also spiritually?

That which should characterize our speech is our love and concern for each other and our desire for each other's spiritual growth. In other words, our communication as married couples ought to reflect the very purpose for which God gave us marriage, to assist one another on the pathway to heaven.

When we speak that which is edifying, we also bring to expression the second purpose in communicating in a spiritually healthy way, namely, that we speak in a way that "may minister grace unto the hearers" (Eph. 4:29). To be able to minister grace means that *you* have been made new by the grace of God that is in Christ Jesus. That means too that the fountain of your speech has been made new. Again, Paul speaks to you who have been called out of darkness, who have been given grace according to the measure of the gift of Christ, as we read in verse 4 of this chapter. In the place of defilement and bitterness and resentment and anger—all of which lie at the heart of rottenness of speech—has been given the awareness of the wonder of God's grace, the peace that has come from hearing his gospel communicated to you in your need, the hope that this gives us in the face of many sorrows. From that fountain of God's grace in your own life comes the desire to minister grace to those whom you love.

Grace, at its very root, is a word that speaks of beauty. The idea, then, is that we want our spouse and our children to be the most spiritually beautiful people that we know. This applies more broadly in the church as well. We want fellow church members to know and to reflect in their lives the wonder of God's grace. We desire that they enjoy in every aspect of life the consciousness that they are an important part of Christ's bride and that they live in the fellowship of his love. We want them to experience that with us.

Glorifying God Together

So we see that belonging to careful communication is the blessedness of glorifying God together. By our conversation we nurture our fellowship and reflect the glory of that covenantal relationship between Christ and his bride. That is the reason for which God has given marriage. That is also the reason he has given us a place in his church. We are not to live in isolation. We are to live in fellowship. We are to teach that also to our children. We are to teach that also by modeling careful communication.

It is important to family life and to the life of the congregation that our homes are those in which we glorify God together. To that end has God saved us. In that way we praise him. Thank God for his faithfulness in communicating to us the gospel of our salvation by the word become flesh. Let us who have heard his word, therefore, minister grace one to another with careful communication.

Chapter 17

WALKING IN THE SPIRIT

This I say then, Walk in the Spirit, and ye shall not fulfil the lust of the flesh.—Galatians 5:16

We have considered careful communication as one of the essentials to living joyfully in marriage. It is interesting that when we look at Galatians 5:16, we find in the immediate context, in verse 15, these words: "But if ye bite and devour one another, take heed that ye be not consumed one of another." Love is to come to expression in careful speech. The lack of love will surely result in a ferocious appetite for biting and devouring one another. What a horrible way to live in any kind of relationship, let alone in marriage. But it is immediately following those words of warning that Paul writes, "This I say then, Walk in the Spirit, and ye shall not fulfil the lust of the flesh" (v. 16).

You will also remember that in the text we considered in the previous chapter, Ephesians 4:29, we were called to careful communication. Immediately following this comes the exhortation, "And grieve not the holy Spirit of God, whereby ye are sealed unto the day of redemption" (v. 30). While the importance of walking in the Spirit is broader than its effects on our speech, there is a relationship between our tongues and our spiritual life that we must give careful attention to.

We are certainly able to conclude by this time that marriage is not only a living and beautiful relationship when we live in the way that God has marked out for us in his word, but that marriage is also a lifelong work. It is not easy work either. But when we are living in close fellowship with our Redeemer, the work invested in our relationships is joyful work and rewarding work.

That said, however, when we consider everything we have seen from Scripture as pertains to the theme of living joyfully in marriage, we can also conclude that we are dealing with something that goes beyond any human capability. If we are going to experience the joy that God intended for us in holy marriage, or the joy that he would have us experience and portray in the midst of the congregation as representative of Christ's bride, that will not come by our own effort. We habitually rob ourselves of that joy. The sin that we bring to expression repeatedly is a clear demonstration of the impossibility of living joyfully apart from the wonder work of the Spirit of the living Christ abiding in us and we in him. So the inspired apostle, that is, the Holy Spirit himself through Paul, calls our attention to our need for walking in the Spirit.

The Experienced Conflict

The text sets before us a conflict that we sorely experience, a conflict that affects every relationship to some degree and that certainly cannot be hidden in marriage, because it is a conflict waged within us. It is the conflict between our flesh and the Spirit.

It is a conflict of which you who are married are well aware. It is a conflict of which you who are not married are also well aware. This conflict is common to every child of God. That explains why, married or not, you have had to confess, "I have not lived in the way that God would have me live. I have not fulfilled my calling as a Christian, or as a Christian husband, or as a Christian wife. How I need Jesus! How I need the forgiveness and the righteousness that

WALKING IN THE SPIRIT

only he can provide!" That is all true. But there is also this: you need the power of that living, exalted Christ to effect the change in your life, in order that laying hold of him by faith, you do experience the joy to which we are called.

The text speaks of one half of the conflict in terms of "the lust of the flesh." The next verse develops the idea of the entire conflict. "For the flesh lusteth against the Spirit, and the Spirit against the flesh: and these are contrary the one to the other: so that ye cannot do the things that ye would" (Gal. 5:17).

Clearly, this means that we are not to expect perfection from each other this side of heaven. We must expect in others, as well as ourselves, that we will be involved in an intense spiritual struggle all our life long.

If you as a husband think you are just fine, and if you as a wife think that there are no personal issues you must address, that any troubles in your marriage are entirely your spouse's fault, then you have a very superficial view of Christianity and a very faulty view of yourself. Our natures remain corrupt, polluted with sin. That is never to be an excuse. That is a reason faithfully to examine ourselves in the light of God's word, to confess our sins before him and one another, and to strive to live in holiness to the glory of our Redeemer. This spiritual conflict is very real and lifelong.

This conflict that each of us must face within ourselves is a conflict that unavoidably affects our marriages, as it does our relationships within Christ's bride the church, insofar as we are not constantly dying to self, weeding our own gardens, and dealing in love one for another. It is a conflict that comes to expression in every sharp word spoken to each other, in every failure to express the love we are called to express, as well as in everything done with a selfish motivation and perspective, to the exclusion of our spouse and without thought to his or her best interests. But above all, this conflict with our flesh comes to expression in our spiritual laziness, our excuses and failures to address the things that need to be changed to glorify God and to better our relationships.

When we as Reformed Christians recognize the sovereignty of God, it is easy to look with a sense of wonder at the way God has led us in life. He determined the parents who would bring us into the world. He determined where we would live growing up and every circumstance in life that would shape our character. He marked out exactly where you would be at this point in your life. For us who are married, God sovereignly determined the way in which we would meet. He gave you the desire for marriage to the particular spouse with whom you are now one. Yes, those ways and desires were often affected by our own sinful lusts, no doubt about it. The Bible exposes us in that. But God himself brought us together. God himself is the one who alone gave us a place among his bride the church. We stand in awe at the wonder of God's sovereignty in our own lives.

But let us remember too that God is the one who determined all our differences. Not only did he make our lives intersect, but he determined everything that makes us different from each other. When we recognize God's sovereignty in these things, we must remember that the reason he brought us together with our differences is that we might reflect in our marriages—and the same is true in our life in the church—the beauty of God's work in taking to himself a bride with tremendous diversity.

All the differences seen in the church, differences in personalities, differences of male and female, different gifts, different ages, social differences, all belong to the beauty of his bride. The same is true in marriage. But we must recognize that God gave us our differences as husbands and wives in order that we might learn to show the beauty of our unity with Christ and with each other, even through our differences. We are not to settle for living in the doldrums in our marriages.

If you face conflicts and struggles, knowing that your marriage is not what it ought to be, you must recognize in a very real sense God's sovereignty in calling you to face these issues. In order to do that, you must answer the question, "Why would God have me struggle this way?"

His purpose is that we experience joy in our marriages and in our Christian lives. Repeatedly the Bible expresses that truth. John put it this way in his first epistle: "These things write we unto you, that your joy may be full" (1 John 1:4). The things that he writes are the blessed truths that reveal our fellowship with God and with one another, the heart of which gospel is the wonder of God's covenant of grace, brought to expression in the divinely established relationship of Christ and the church.

If you should have to ask the question, "Why would God have me struggle this way?" the answer is that you might step back and examine your relationship to him and to one another, and that you might respond to the wonder of the gospel in a way that promotes the unity and fellowship you are called to express. He would have you look again at the relationship of Christ and the church, at the way in which Christ expresses his love for his bride; he would have you look at the proper response of his bride, and all that in the consciousness of what Jesus Christ has done and is doing by his ongoing work of redemption.

If you are a child of God, the power of sin has been broken in your life. The proclamation of Romans 6:11 must ring in your ears and reverberate through your mind: "Likewise reckon ye also yourselves to be dead indeed unto sin, but alive unto God through Jesus Christ our Lord." Yes, we still have a sin problem. We still have a sinful nature to deal with. It is not just the sinful nature of your spouse. It is not even especially the sinful nature of your spouse. You must realize and confess, "The sin problem is my own. The sinful nature I have to deal with is my own sinful nature."

Notice, Paul speaks in terms of fulfilling the lust of the flesh.

Fulfilling. The idea there is one of putting the finishing touches on what began as a desire. We must realize, in other words, the seriousness of letting our lust have its way. Lust is the power of our depraved nature drawing us toward that which is contrary to God's will. It is the power that would have us take even a good gift of God and make it vile by putting it to the service of self, instead of using it to the glory of God.

A man or woman who fails to exercise self-control is one soon given over to the lust of the flesh. That comes to expression in addictions of many different types. How many have destroyed their lives, even the lives of their families, by fulfilling the lust of the flesh? How many have destroyed their health, as well as their spiritual health, by fulfilling the lust of the flesh?

Do you need to be reminded how serious it is to let your lust have its way? "But every man is tempted, when he is drawn away of his own lust, and enticed. Then when lust hath conceived, it bringeth forth sin: and sin, when it is finished, bringeth forth death" (James 1:14–15). That is how serious it is to let your lust have its way. If you are a child of God, you do not want to fulfill the lust of the flesh. You want your life to be an expression of the freedom from sin and the joy that is yours in the fellowship of God by the power of Christ's redemption and work in your life. So how are you going to overcome that lust? How are you going to resolve those sins that you realize are robbing you of the joy you should be experiencing as a child of God? The text gives us the answer. It is an important admonition that provides the key to a joyful Christian life and, for those who are married, a joyful life with the spouse God has given.

The Important Admonition

The admonition is this: "Walk in the Spirit." Any hope of subduing the sinful expression of our natures is found only in this: walking in the Spirit.

Understand that Paul addresses those who are redeemed. He speaks to you who are conscious of the battle because it is part of your own experience. The testimony of Romans 7 is real to you. If you think that the problem is everyone else's, that you do not have a problem, then this text is not for you. It is not for you because there is no spiritual life in you. You have yet to see the seriousness of your own sin before the holy and righteous God who demands perfect love all the time. You have yet to come to true repentance. The Spirit of Christ has not yet worked that grace in you. But if you know very well your own faults as before the face of the perfectly holy God, your sins and the sinfulness of your nature—which the devil also knows and attacks—if you have been given by the Spirit the grace of repentance, if you are sorry for your sins, then to you comes the admonition, "Walk in the Spirit."

This is a reminder to us that our marriages, as well as our lives in the midst of Christ's church, are lived as part of the process of sanctification. As we have seen, marriage is given to a man and a woman that they might help one another on the pathway to heaven. When we understand that, as we have seen from Scripture, then we can also understand marriage as serving God's design for our spiritual growth in holiness. But marriage serves that designed purpose only in conjunction with our walking in the Spirit. After all, any spiritual growth in holiness only comes by the Holy Spirit who works holiness in those who belong to Christ.

We have considered various conflicts that affect our marriages, conflicts all rooted in the idolatry of self. That is what the lust of the flesh is all about. It does not matter what different kinds of struggles you have experienced or do experience right now. It might be conflict of all different sorts. It might be your struggle with addiction, whether it be to substance abuse, to power, to your technological devices or online gaming. Maybe it is pornography that separates you from God and from your spouse.

The lust of the flesh comes to expression in many different ways. In the churches of Galatia there were all kinds of arguments and disputes and church-destroying bickering. Paul was addressing the same kinds of things that are found in some homes within the church today.

The point is this: if you think that you are going to be able to settle the disputes, have victory in the battle, and find peace and joy in your relationship; if you think you are going to be able to overcome your addiction and personal sins while you continue to neglect your spiritual life, you are sadly mistaken and foolish. You cannot live in separation from the Holy Spirit and experience joy and peace that are the blessings of that Holy Spirit.

This text, in its context, emphasizes that the solution to our problems, the way to a joyful life in the relationships God gives us, is not to be found in a superficial do-good philosophy, nor the self-help solutions that are the proclamations of not only the world of psychology but much of the evangelical church world of our day. The power of a joyful Christianity, the source of a joyful marriage, is to be found in a walk by faith in Christ that lays hold of God's word by the power of the Holy Spirit.

This text calls us to beware of a Christ-less Christianity. That is really the emphasis of the apostle in the context. He is emphasizing in this epistle to the Galatians the dangers of the bondage of legalism and setting forth the beautiful contrast of the freedom that is ours in Christ Jesus. That freedom, though, is not a freedom to serve ourselves. Never may Christian liberty be construed as the freedom to do what I please, to serve my own lust. Christian liberty is the freedom to walk in the Spirit, the freedom to serve our Lord Jesus in heartfelt thankfulness. It is the freedom of being broken from the bondage to self and to the sin in which we were once enslaved. It is the freedom to serve one another in love and to reflect in that way the life of Christ in us.

In the Christian church today, there is all too much error that departs from the balanced presentation of the Bible concerning what it means to have life in Christ.

There is the danger, ever present in the church, represented by the life of the Pharisees of Jesus' day, that would make the Christian life consist in the external things, governed not by what the word of God says, but by men's opinions of what the word of God says. That is why I caution repeatedly, also to our children in catechism classes: Do not take what I say just because I say it. Let's see it as a faithful exposition of the word of God. His alone, after all, is the authority to tell us what to believe and how to live.

But the other danger today, and far broader by my observation, is the loss of the antithesis and the idea that so long as we are *spiritual*, we can pretty much live as we please. The spirituality of much of the Christian church today is a feel-good religion in which they can say, "The Spirit made me feel this way," or "The Spirit told me this is what I should do." I have had people attempt to justify their walk in sin by such a claim. I have had to remind them that the Spirit never contradicts what he tells us in the holy Scriptures, and that "the voice that told you to walk in such a way was either the voice of your own deceitful heart or the voice of Satan, but it was not the voice of the Spirit of Christ."

If you are one who takes the attitude, "Well, my marriage doesn't give me a lot of joy, but I'm not going to change and I don't need to change, because I believe in Jesus and I'm saved," then I have to tell you, "You are still in bondage." The true freedom of the Christian life comes not by Jesus saving us in spite of our continuing to live as if that salvation makes no difference. True freedom, the freedom of being saved by Christ, is freedom *from* sin, freedom to *do* the will of God and therefore to experience the joy that he gives to those who love him.

To live with a "so what" attitude is a demonstration of one who is still in bondage, not having been made free by the Holy Spirit. Jesus said in John 8:34, "Verily, verily, I say unto you"—notice the emphasis there—"Whosoever committeth sin"—that speaks of ongoing action, of continuing to live in the lust of the flesh, be it in the form of biting and devouring one another or anything else contrary to the precepts of God—"is the servant"—the slave—"of sin."

Do you belong to your faithful Savior Jesus Christ? Then Paul speaks to you: "Walk in the Spirit, and ye shall not fulfill the lust of the flesh."

What does it mean to walk in the Spirit?

It means, first, that we walk with the Spirit every day. The apostle calls us to ongoing action. If you are going to attempt to get by in fellowship with the Spirit only on Sunday, you will not and cannot enjoy the fruit of the Spirit in your daily life. Is Sunday a special day? Absolutely! We enter the joy of our Lord especially during that day in which he speaks to us by the word preached. But to walk in the Spirit is a call to daily action, to a conscious and humble dependence upon the Spirit and his guidance.

To walk in the Spirit means, second, that we are to walk as he guides us. Let's immediately understand, the Spirit guides us by the word of the Scriptures. It is a counterfeit spirituality that ignores the Bible and talks about feelings. The Holy Spirit always leads us to Christ as Lord, the one who owns us and therefore who rules us. The Spirit leads us to Christ by Christ's *word*, applying that word to our minds and hearts and lives and working in us a godly submission to our Lord. The Spirit makes us willing to do what the Scriptures require of us.

That means, to put it bluntly, if you are not willing to put in the effort to conform your life to the word of God, your Christianity is a fraud. You are not walking in the Spirit. You might be *spiritual*, as the world looks upon that term. You might be as religious as the Pharisees. But do not deceive yourself. You are not walking in the

Spirit when you are not willing to do what the Scriptures require of you.

If walking in the Spirit includes the willingness to do what God requires of us in his word and to walk by faith in his covenantal fellowship, then it also means that we want to grow in our understanding of his word and in the knowledge of who he is for us and the wonder work of what he has done for us. We want to grow in the sense of awe that we have for him.

Furthermore, because God created us to live not as individuals but in community, he would have us grow in our knowledge of him not just as individuals, but as belonging to the covenantal family that he has formed and is forming in Christ Jesus. He created us for the relationship, the bond of fellowship and love, that defines the covenant. We can talk about personal responsibility, and that is very real. But there is also something very wrong about the attitude, "I'll pull myself up by my own bootstraps," meaning, "I'll improve my circumstances on my own." To walk in the Spirit is to live in the fellowship of God's people, the church. It is to live as members of Christ's bride!

I can understand the desire on the part of some to isolate themselves. Various factors might contribute to that desire. There are times in my own life when I would just as soon isolate myself. But the Bible makes clear that you cannot grow in your Christian life, you cannot grow in sanctification, if you live in isolation. You cannot because that isolation is contrary to the very purpose of God in saving you.

That means, if you find difficulties in your life or in your marriage and you are going to attempt to deal with those difficulties while ignoring God's word in the fellowship of his people, you are making one foolish and futile attempt. It is troubling when people in Christ's church require counseling to deal with various problems, even sins within marriage, but refuse to attend the Bible studies of the church and continue to live on the fringes of the congregation in isolation from most of the people of God. That is foolishness! God will not let you live in isolation from the body of Christ and experience the joy of his fellowship. He will not reward your spiritual neglect and disobedience. "This I say then, Walk in the Spirit, and ye shall not fulfill the lust of the flesh." Walk in the Spirit, who works by the word within the fellowship of God's people, the church.

Finally (and more might be said about the concept of walking in the Spirit, but I conclude with this), walking in the Spirit means also that we flee temptation. That means, for one thing, we avoid that which would draw out the lust of the flesh. If your inappropriate use of that smartphone has damaged the necessary time for communication with your spouse, and that device has such a hold on you that you are unable to break yourself from its enticement, then you best take a sledgehammer to that device, break it into a million pieces, and buy yourself a cheap, no-frill flip phone for being able to make calls when necessary.

You are aware too of what the Bible tells us concerning lust when it issues the call of God, "Flee fornication." You cannot walk in the Spirit when you continue to live as close to sin as possible. You cannot walk in the Spirit when, as one who struggles with addiction, you continue to think that perhaps you can have "just a little." Sanctification does not work that way! To walk in the Spirit is to flee that which would draw us into fulfilling the lust of the flesh. It is to do so by so filling our life with the fullness of Christ, that we crowd out all the garbage.

We also must understand the power of the word of God in calling us to walk in the Spirit. I am not the one issuing the call, "Walk in the Spirit." My words could accomplish nothing. Nor is this a call to self-help. There are certain actions we can take to benefit ourselves in many different ways. But when it comes to our spiritual life and sanctification, we look to the sovereignty of God and his work. The call that comes to us in the gospel, the call that at its heart is the call to repentance and faith, is a call that *Christ* speaks and that his Spirit applies powerfully and irresistibly to you who are his. He not only says, "Walk in the Spirit," but he gives you the freedom and the power to do exactly that. He works in us both "to will and to do of his good pleasure" (Phil. 2:12–13).

The Certain Consequence

The consequence of walking in the Spirit is that we experience the joy of the fellowship of our heavenly Father in Jesus Christ and the awareness of his blessing also in the relationships he has given us.

Once again, it is important to remember that this conflict into which we have been thrust is a conflict that comes as the fruit of the Spirit's work. Without regeneration, there is no conflict with the lust of the flesh. We simply seek to fulfill that lust and consume ourselves in the process with all measure of sorrows. It is only by God having given us the life of Christ that we have become new creatures, who recognize with sorrow the sinfulness of our own natures. It is only by the wonder work of God's grace, sovereign and irresistible grace, that we have been called out of darkness into his marvelous light. But he has done so, giving us to see that we are not our own. Christ bore our punishment and freed us from the bondage of sin and death, that we might live unto him.

It is this wonder of the life-giving Spirit that gives hope to any marriage that has not been what it should be. That work of God's grace, wrought by the power of his word, is what gives us the understanding that we are not ensnared in the bondage of our sorrows and conflict, in whatever expression those sorrows may take.

We have the hope that, living in the Spirit, we not only may but shall enjoy the kind of marriage or relationship in Christ's church that God calls us to enjoy. For we are able to see in our lives the certain consequence of our loving and faithful Redeemer, the bridegroom of the church, leading us faithfully toward heaven and giving us the fullness of joy of living in his fellowship *together* as husbands and wives and as members of Christ's bride.

Chapter 18

ON YOUR
KNEES TOGETHER

That your prayers be not hindered.—1 Peter 3:7

I call your attention to the concluding essential to living joyfully
in marriage. That I treat this last is not in any sense indicative of
it being less important than what we have considered to this point.
In a very real sense prayer is the most important essential to a joyful
marriage. But I treat it at this place in the book because it quite
naturally follows what we considered in the last chapter, our need to
walk in the Spirit.

As Christians we are entirely dependent upon the Spirit of the
exalted Christ for a healthy spiritual life. For those who are married,
a healthy spiritual life is the very foundation for a healthy, joyful
marriage. Because the Spirit works through the word, we must live
before the word of God always, subjecting ourselves to the teaching of the Scriptures, particularly with application to our own lives
and the decisions that we must face. We must do so living in the
consciousness of the wonder of the gospel, seen in the relationship
between Christ and his bride the church.

But if there is one thing Scripture emphasizes in that relationship that is ours with Christ, and with the Father through Jesus

Christ, it is our dependence upon him in everything. Not only does our understanding of the gospel and of the covenant of grace compel us to heartfelt gratitude to God, but it also compels us to humble ourselves before his divine majesty and the wonder of his grace in taking us into the fellowship of his life and love through Jesus Christ our Lord.

Prayer, as the Heidelberg Catechism sets before us from Scripture in Lord's Day 45, "is the chief part of thankfulness which God requires of us." But also pointed out in that Lord's Day is the fact that "God will give his grace and Holy Spirit to those only who with sincere desires continually ask them of him, and are thankful for them."[1] If we desire that our marriages, and even our lives in the midst of Christ's bride the church, reflect the glory of the relationship between Christ and his bride, if we desire to live joyfully in marriage, that desire must be expressed to God in prayer. It must be expressed not occasionally or rarely, but continually and with regularity. Our desire must be expressed continually out of thankfulness for the relationship into which God has taken us in our marriage to Christ.

Essential to living joyfully in marriage is that we spend time on our knees together as husbands and wives. Essential to living joyfully in Christ's church is that we spend time on our knees together.

There is yet another reason to treat the matter of prayer last in our list of essentials to living joyfully in marriage. While it can be said that prayer is essential to a healthy spiritual life, another perspective comes out in the context of the text that we consider in this connection. There are two references to prayer in 1 Peter 3. You will also find a third reference to prayer in chapter 4:7. In the three you find one thing in common. They do not point to prayer as the key to living right. But they all reflect on the importance of living in godliness to a healthy prayer life. To live in obedience to God in

---

1   Heidelberg Catechism A 116, in *Confessions and Church Order*, 134.

all the other things we have contemplated in this book as our calling in marriage, or as members of Christ's bride, is the only way we will also find communion with God in prayer. That too provides a reason for taking this matter of prayer as our concluding consideration of living joyfully in marriage.

As I call your attention to the last clause of 1 Peter 3:7, "that your prayers be not hindered," notice the positive implication of that expression, namely, that belonging to a healthy marriage and to the joy of marriage is regular and consistent time on your knees together.

The Great Necessity

That a husband and wife pray together is necessary. When a husband and wife stand before the calling to live as one, and therefore as best friends, reflecting the covenantal relationship between Christ and his bride, it is understood that communication is an essential part of that unity. We who have been made members of Christ's bride, we who have been taken into the fellowship of his life and love by the wonder of divine grace and the Spirit of adoption, also find communication with him a necessary part of our lives as his people. We communicate with him through prayer. We communicate openly with him, we pour out our heart before him (Ps. 62:8), because we trust in him, knowing his great love for us. We praise him. We thank him. We express our dependence upon him. We confide in him and bring our requests to him. We pray together as husband and wife. We begin our days with personal prayer. We pray together around the table. If God gives us children, we have devotions together with them, teaching them also the importance of prayer in our lives. We pray regularly.

Yes, our heavenly Father requires prayer from us. Repeatedly in Scripture he calls us to prayer. But that call to prayer is similar to what you might say to your daughter if she is standing with bad posture. She stands; but you say to her, "Stand up straight. It's not good to slouch." We pray, but we must be reminded repeatedly to pray *properly*, to think about what we pray.

It is not my purpose here to develop the concept of proper prayer. That is unfolded for us by the Heidelberg Catechism in its treatment of the Lord's prayer, where Jesus gave us the specific requirements of the prayer that is acceptable to God and that he will hear. There he carefully spelled out for us both how we should approach God and for what we should pray.

But as we consider the last clause of 1 Peter 3:7, it is important that we understand why praying together is a necessary and very important aspect of married life.

Let's reflect on why prayer is necessary.

First, God requires that we live as thankful Christians. Prayer, being the chief part of thankfulness, is the necessary expression of our gratitude for what God has given us in taking us into the fellowship of his life and covenantal family.

We are not very good at expressing thanks. We take so many things for granted. We do that with each other. How often do you thank each other? How often do you thank your wife for this and that particular labor she performs? Do you simply take for granted those meals that she prepares? Do you take her housekeeping for granted? Do you take for granted all those diapers she changes and the care she provides for your children? Do you say, "Well, after all, that's her job"? And you wives, do you take for granted your husband's labors to provide for you? Do you take for granted the upkeep of your home? Do you take for granted the time he spends with the children and the occasional breaks he gives you? Do you simply regard that as his calling and therefore something that does not require your thanks?

It is bad enough that we take each other for granted, but dare we take anything for granted when we stand before our heavenly

Father? Do you thank him for the absolute wonder of his grace in saving you? Do you thank him for the fact that he, before whom the nations of the world are but the dust of the balance, has looked upon you in his eternal love? Do you thank him that he has taken such a sinner as you and cleansed you and forgiven you, even at the cost of the life of his only begotten Son? And look at your life. Do you thank your heavenly Father for the place he has given you in his own covenantal family, as a member of Christ's bride? Do you? Do you thank him for the treasures he has entrusted to you in his gospel, in holy Scripture? Do you thank him that though you differ not at all by nature from the multitudes of unbelievers and ungodly in this world, yet he has looked upon you in the face of his own dear Son? Do you thank him for the way in which he has led you to this point in your life? After all, we confess as the Bible teaches us that he works all things together for our good, that everything in your life and mine serves the purpose of our heavenly Father to lead us to the inheritance he has prepared for us as those whom he has saved. Do you thank him for your brothers and sisters in Christ, the fellow members of Christ's bride? If you are married, do you look at your spouse and thank God?

Some have sinned in taking a spouse without seeking the will of God, even in disobedience to him. But in the process of much pain and sorrow, God has brought them to repentance and called them unto himself and to the rich fellowship of the marriage of Christ and the church that earthly marriages can only faintly reflect. Do you thank God, then, for what he has done in your life, even using the painful experiences to draw you to himself?

For you who have a godly spouse—a fellow sinner, yes, but one redeemed by Christ, one who loves him and his word and thus strives to live as expressing that love—do you thank God for that spouse? We have considered the fact that marriage is but a temporary earthly relationship that God has given until death parts us, a relationship that serves us in our spiritual sojourn. Do you thank God for your spouse?

If he has given you children, the privilege of bringing forth and nurturing his children, do you thank him for that?

I mention but a few things for which we owe God our thanks. Do we express to him that thankfulness in our prayers? Or do we, in horrible ingratitude, take all these things for granted?

Second, belonging to the necessity of prayer and flowing from our thankful consideration of who God is and what he has done for us is the fact that we understand our complete dependence upon him and his divine grace.

When you stand before your calling as a Christian recognizing the human impossibility of the life God calls you to live, when you stand before your calling as a Christian husband or a Christian wife and you consider what God requires of you properly to reflect the relationship of Christ and the church, the *love* that he requires to be exercised perfectly toward him and one another, then you certainly recognize the human impossibility of fulfilling that calling. Do you seek God's grace and the spiritual strength that can only come from him? Do you look to him to supply you with what is necessary to live according to his will? Do you make that a matter of fervent prayer? Do you truly seek his will? Do you acknowledge that his alone is the power, to be worked by the Holy Spirit in your life, to give you what is necessary to experience the joy of marriage that is his purpose? Or do you set out to do it on your own, only to find the futility of such efforts? Do you seek to handle your finances without regard to the will of God, without making his will a matter of prayer? Do you truly seek from him your daily bread, or in your estimation is that something you can well take care of on your own?

Prayer is necessary because you and I are dependent upon our heavenly Father and our exalted bridegroom for everything. To seek his will, therefore, is our calling. We are to express that also in our prayers, even as Jesus taught us.

Third, prayer is necessary because we must face our sin and we must do so before him whom we have offended so greatly. As Christian husbands and wives, but also as members of Christ's bride, we have seen not only how far short we have fallen, but how absolutely sinful we have been! We have lived as rebels in God's house! We have sinned against each other by our failures to live in the way that God has called us to live. In sinning against each other we have sinned against and greatly offended God himself. Would you not confess that before him in the godly sorrow of repentance?

Belonging to the necessity of prayer is our need to confess our sins before God, in order to receive from him the forgiveness that he alone can give. That forgiveness, after all, is critical to the consciousness of God's fellowship with us and therefore to the joy that is ours only in that fellowship with our Redeemer. Because he forgives us only insofar as we forgive one another, we need also to pray for grace to look upon one another as standing together beneath the cross of our Lord Jesus Christ, and to confess our sins one to another as well.

Finally, prayer is necessary for us because in marriage we face many trials and sorrows. What is common to us all in our walk through this fallen world is magnified in such a close relationship as marriage and family life. We bear each other's burdens.

The trials that we face in marriage and family life are innumerable. God mercifully gives them only incrementally, recognizing the limitations of what we can bear. Some of you have gone through excruciating trials together. Some walk through them now. Mothers soon learned what a tremendously difficult calling is the care of small children. Parents have taken their little ones to the hospital. There have been times when we helplessly watched our loved ones suffer. We have carried the burdens of each other's sins. Some parents have carried the grief of wayward children.

In all the various trials we have faced and continue to experience together, we are reminded again and again how helpless we are apart from the sustaining grace of God our Father. He would have us pour out our hearts before him, cast our cares upon him. Through all those things he has shown himself merciful, also in drawing us closer to him through prayer. So the great necessity of being on our knees together in prayer presses upon us from several different perspectives, all of which would have us stand in awe before God and his love for us in Christ Jesus.

The Terrible Hindrances

The text we consider also indicates that there are terrible hindrances to our prayer life that we must constantly remove from our lives. The word *hindered* is a violent term, expressing the damage that is caused to our prayer life. It speaks of a cutting injury to our fellowship with God. It describes us taking a knife, as it were, and swiping at our prayer life and cutting a deep gash into it. We stand in proud rebellion before God and live as if we do not need him. We neglect the callings that he gives us and fail to bring to expression the love that he demands of us. In doing so, we sever ourselves from him who is our life, our strength, and the only source of our joy. After all, as we are warned in Proverbs 28:9, "He that turneth away his ear from hearing the law, even his prayer shall be abomination."

First Peter 3:7 ties prayer to the calling of the husband. The husband, in his calling to represent Christ, is the head of the home, the spiritual leader. Belonging to that headship is his calling to guide and direct his wife and household spiritually. He is to be the chief prophet in the home, leading his family into the word of God and proclaiming that gospel to the application of his household. He is to rule in the authority of that word as he represents Christ as king. Belonging to that spiritual headship of the husband is also the priestly aspect of his office, leading his family to the throne of grace in prayer, also intercessory prayer.

It is the natural unfolding of the biblical doctrine of marriage, therefore, that Peter would speak of prayer in connection with the husband's calling.

Not to be overlooked is the fact that he speaks specifically of the husband's calling toward his wife as that which affects the prayer life of the home. If a husband fails to live with his wife according to the calling God has given him, if he does not dwell with her in a way that reflects Christ's covenantal relationship with his bride, if the husband does not honor his wife, understanding the support and care she needs as the weaker vessel, he will be unable to pray with her and for her as is his calling.

While the emphasis here is on the husband, simply because of the high calling God has given him as the representative of Christ in the marriage covenant, the same holds true of the wife who is disobedient to the calling God has given her. She who lives contrary to the word of God in marriage cannot express the fellowship that God expects of us in prayer.

The same is true with your place and mine in the midst of the church as members of the bride of Christ. We have been taught to pray recognizing our relationship together. We have been taught to pray, "*Our* Father...give *us*...forgive *us*," and so on. If we are not living in the unity God has established and that he calls us to express, our prayers are hindered. If either of us—husband or wife—is going to insist always on having it his or her own way, if we are not going to listen carefully to each other, if we are not going to live with a forgiving spirit, then we are not going to be able to pray together either, "Forgive *us*." You cannot pray for *us* when life to you is all about *me*, about self.

The calling that stands before us concerning our prayer life is immediately set forth by the apostle in the following two verses, 1

Peter 3:8–9, with application not just to married couples but to the whole church, members of Christ's bride:

8. Finally, be ye all of one mind [that is, live in the unity of the joy of the gospel, the unity of the Spirit of truth], having compassion one of another, love as brethren, be pitiful, be courteous:

9. Not rendering evil for evil, or railing for railing: but contrariwise blessing; knowing that ye are thereunto called, that ye should inherit a blessing.

All these positive callings are expressions of love, as we have seen. They are expressions of the life of Christ in us. That is why being on your knees together goes hand in hand with faithfulness to God in all the other aspects of your married life. How important therefore is the calling God has given us as husbands, as wives, as members of Christ's bride. How crucial that we be not merely hearers of the word, but doers also (James 1:22).

The Blessed Fruitfulness

Then we shall experience the blessed fruitfulness of that time on our knees together. To pray together strengthens the cord that is your covenantal relationship together. It strengthens your relationship because it draws you together to Christ in that "threefold cord [that] is not quickly broken" (Eccl. 4:12). It gives a taste of that perfect fellowship we shall enjoy with our bridegroom in heaven, where all the members of Christ's bride shall praise God together in the perfect joy of his presence. Isn't that our desire?

To have our relationship strengthened by fellowship with our Redeemer is the very purpose for which God gave us each other. Whether we talk about our place in the church or in marriage, God gave us to each other to help one another, to build up each other, to strengthen the bond of our relationship together, "Till we all come in the unity of the faith, and of the knowledge of the Son of God, unto a perfect man, unto the measure of the stature of the fulness of Christ," as Paul writes in Ephesians 4:13. To be on our knees together, to be a prayerful people, also in our homes, is to enjoy the blessed fruitfulness of being partakers of Christ and all his benefits.

Prayer, exercised together in the presence of God and in fellowship with him through Christ our bridegroom, bears above all the joy of knowing that we are partakers of his grace and Holy Spirit. What an amazing thing that such sinners as we are able to go into the tabernacle where God dwells! That Christ has taken me as a member of his bride is absolutely mind-boggling! That Christ has established such gospel intimacy with me, shedding his love abroad in my heart, is amazing! Do you live in the consciousness of that wonder?

To live in the joy of the gospel is the heart of the Christian life. To live in the joy of the gospel is what God would have us bring to expression also in our marriages.

God is in the midst of us! He is in the midst of our marriages. Call upon him. Rely on him. Live in the joy of the fellowship of his love. Confess your sins before him and seek from him the grace also to bring to expression in your life and in your marriage the joy of the gospel. And know that he hears and answers the prayers of those who come to him in Jesus Christ. He hears and answers the prayers of husbands and wives who come on their knees together.